Simon Oberthür

Towards an RTOS for Self-optimizing Mechatronic Systems

Simon Oberthür

Towards an RTOS for Self-optimizing Mechatronic Systems

**Südwestdeutscher Verlag für
Hochschulschriften**

Imprint
Any brand names and product names mentioned in this book are subject to trademark, brand or patent protection and are trademarks or registered trademarks of their respective holders. The use of brand names, product names, common names, trade names, product descriptions etc. even without a particular marking in this work is in no way to be construed to mean that such names may be regarded as unrestricted in respect of trademark and brand protection legislation and could thus be used by anyone.

Publisher:
Südwestdeutscher Verlag für Hochschulschriften
is a trademark of
Dodo Books Indian Ocean Ltd., member of the OmniScriptum S.R.L Publishing group
str. A.Russo 15, of. 61, Chisinau-2068, Republic of Moldova Europe
Printed at: see last page
ISBN: 978-3-8381-2668-5

Zugl. / Approved by: Paderborn, Universität, Diss., 2009

Copyright © Simon Oberthür
Copyright © 2011 Dodo Books Indian Ocean Ltd., member of the OmniScriptum S.R.L Publishing group

Towards an RTOS for Self-optimizing Mechatronic Systems

Dissertation

A thesis submitted to the
Faculty of Computer Science, Electrical Engineering and Mathematics
of the
University of Paderborn
in partial fulfillment of the requirements for the
degree of *Dr. rer. nat.*

Simon Oberthür

Paderborn, Germany
October 30, 2009

Contents

Abstract   v

I. Preamble   1

1. Summary   3

2. Introduction   7
    2.1. Aim of this Thesis 8
    2.2. Classification into the State of the Art 9
    2.3. Organisation of this Thesis 10
    2.4. Overview of Publications of the Author Related to this Thesis 12

II. Foundations and Related Work   13

3. Self-optimization   15
    3.1. Collaborative Research Center 614 15
    3.2. Definition of Self-Optimization 16
    3.3. Objectives and System of Objectives 17
    3.4. Architecture of the Information Processing of Self-Optimizing Systems 17
    3.5. Multi-stage Dependability Concept 19
    3.6. Platform for Self-Optimizing Applications 20
    3.7. Design of Self-optimizing Systems 22
    3.8. Demonstrators of the Collaborative Research Center 614 22
       3.8.1. Active Suspension System 23
       3.8.2. Self-optimizing Drive Control 28
       3.8.3. Operating Point Assignment 29
    3.9. Requirements of Self-Optimizing Applications 31

	3.9.1. Summarized Requirements to the System Software	33
3.10.	Chapter Conclusion	33

4. Real-time Operating Systems and Resource Management — 35

4.1.	RTOS Classification	36
	4.1.1. Real-time Extensions for Commercial Operating Systems	36
	4.1.2. Component-based Real-Time Operating Systems	37
	4.1.3. QoS-based Real-Time Operating Systems	37
	4.1.4. Reflective Operating Systems	38
	4.1.5. Resource Kernel	39
4.2.	Real-time Scheduling	40
	4.2.1. Earliest Deadline First	41
	4.2.2. Total Bandwidth Server	42
4.3.	Engineering Standards	43
4.4.	Chapter conclusion	45

III. RTOS for Self-optimizing Mechatronic Systems - The Concepts — 47

5. The Flexible Resource Manager - Concept — 49

5.1.	General System Model	49
	5.1.1. Task	50
	5.1.2. Resources	50
5.2.	Flexible Resource Manager	52
	5.2.1. Profile Definition	52
	5.2.2. Profile Configuration	55
	5.2.3. Quality of the System	57
	5.2.4. Profile Reachability Graph	57
	5.2.5. Allowing Over-Allocation	58
	5.2.6. Dynamic of Profile Values	58
5.3.	Comparison to Mode Change Protocols	59
5.4.	The FRM - A Self Optimizing System	60
5.5.	Chapter Conclusion	60

6. The Flexible Resource Manager - Analysis — 63

6.1.	Scheduling of Profile Reconfiguration	63

	6.1.1. Analyzing Guaranteed Configurations	65
	6.1.2. Analyzing Reconfiguration Due to Optimization	66
	6.1.3. Analyzing Reconfiguration Due to Exhaustion	67
6.2.	Analysis for Deadlock Freeness	77
6.3.	Chapter Conclusion	80

7. The Flexible Resource Manager - Optimization   81
    7.1. Event Prediction 82
    7.2. Finding a Good Profile Configuration 87
    7.3. Chapter Conclusion 89

8. Building a Self-Optimizing RTOS   91
    8.1. The RTOS DREAMS 92
       8.1.1. TEReCS 92
    8.2. From Offline TEReCS to Online TEReCS 94
    8.3. Integration of TEReCS and the FRM into the RTOS 97
    8.4. SORTOS - Case Study 101
    8.5. Chapter Conclusion 104

9. Application Design Flow   107
    9.1. Extended Modeling 107
    9.2. Profile Synthesis 109
    9.3. Case Study 117
    9.4. Chapter Conclusion 118

IV. RTOS for Self-optimizing Mechatronic Systems - Evaluation   119

10. Case Studies   121
    10.1. Active Suspension System 121
    10.2. Self-optimizing Drive Control 123
    10.3. Acute Stress Response in Resource Management 124
       10.3.1. Operating Point Assignment and the Acute Stress Response 126
    10.4. Chapter Conclusion 128

11. Simulation   129
    11.1. The TrueTime and MATLAB/Simulink Based Simulator 129

11.2. Evaluation Using Case Studies 132
  11.2.1. Interaction Between the Applications 135
 11.3. Evaluation Using Randomized Simulation 140
 11.4. Chapter Conclusion 143

V. Conclusion and Outlook 145

12. Conclusion and Outlook 147
 12.1. Conclusion 147
 12.2. Outlook 149
 12.3. Look-ahead Optimization 149
 12.4. Advanced Profiles for Flexible Ressource Management 151
  12.4.1. Advanced FRM Profiling 151

Bibliography 153

Abstract

The next generation of advanced mechatronic systems is expected to behave more intelligently than today's systems. They adjust their goals and behavior according to changes of the environment or system. An approach to reach this goal is the concept of self-optimization. Characteristic for these modern applications are the increasing dynamics. To handle this dynamics new approaches in the underlying system software are required.

In general, mechatronic systems are embedded software systems with hard real-time requirements. Predictability is of paramount importance for these systems. Thus, their design has to take the worst-case into account and the maximum required resources are usually allocated upfront by each process. This is safe, but usually results in a rather poor resource utilization.

For a better utilization of the system the Flexible Resource Manager – developed in this thesis – puts temporarily unused resources at other applications' disposal. To consume freed resources the applications can specify additional modes (called profiles) with higher resource consumptions. The state, when resources which are reserved for applications worst-case requirements are put to other applications' disposal, is called over-allocation. To allow over-allocation under hard real-time constrains an acceptance test is checking, if a possible conflict can be solved without violating deadlines of hard real-time tasks. An atomic reconfiguration process is necessary, with the constraint that no hard timing constraint is violated. Thus, the deadline assignment rule of the Total Bandwidth Server (TBS) to schedule reconfiguration is reused for the acceptance test.

This approach is also applied to the operating system itself in this thesis. The resource usage implies the services that the applications require from the operating system. Thus, the operating system must either provide all services that are totally required over time or reconfigure itself. Reconfiguration of the operating system means supporting on demand services or the possibility of degrading services. An approach is presented where an offline customizable operating system is extended in order to be dynamically reconfigurable during run-time. Additionally, the procedure is described how the operating system is aware of the current required services.

To enable an easy integration in the design of modern mechatronic systems a semi-automatic method is described to generate multi-mode applications out of hybrid state charts. Additionally, a Matlab/Simulink based simulator is presented for integration of the resource management approach

Abstract

in the early design phases in this thesis. Case studies are presented to complete the thesis and depict the added value, when using the presented approaches.

Part I.

Preamble

1. Summary

The next generation of advanced mechatronic systems is expected to behave more intelligently than today's systems. An approach to build these systems is to use the concept of self-optimization. Within this approach the systems adjust their goals and behavior according to changes of the environment. Thus, modern self-optimizing mechatronic systems have highly dynamic resource consumption. Common real-time systems and middleware software are too fixed and not optimal for such scenarios. Thus, these layers must adapt themselves to the changing requirements of the application layer.

A problem with dynamic real-time applications using common real-time system software is that applications allocate resources up to their maximum requirements. On the one hand, this allocation behavior guarantees that the applications have all resources being required during execution. On the other hand, the maximum resources are often required only in the worst case and are unused most of the time.

In this thesis a Flexible Resource Manager (FRM) is presented, which permits an over-allocation of resources under hard real-time constrains. The technique allows to minimize the internal waste of resources by putting temporarily unused, but reserved for the worst-case, resources at other applications' disposal. Additionally, an adaptive self-optimizing system or middleware software can be build using this technique.

To use the Flexible Resource Manager applications have to stick to a specific resource allocation paradigm and can specify multiple modes of operation – so called profiles – to allocate additional resources if other applications temporarily do not need them. The resource allocation paradigm comprises:

1. The application has to specify *a priori* the minimum and maximum limits per *resource usage*. The application cannot acquire less or more resources than specified in the current active profile, which the FRM activates. If the application wants to do so, then it has to specify a new profile with appropriate limits. The activation of the new profile underlies an *acceptance test* of the FRM.

2. The FRM is in charge of the assignment of applications into their profiles. If a reconfiguration between profiles is enforced by the FRM, application-specific transition functions are activated.

This allows an application-specific change between different operation modes with different resource requirements.

3. The FRM also registers the actual resource consumption of the active profile of an application, which must be within the specified limits. The FRM guarantees to the applications that they can allocate the resources up to the specified limit in the active profiles. In case of a resource conflict – when the system is over-allocated – the FRM solves the conflict by forcing applications into other profiles so that every resource request can be fulfilled. The FRM injures that no deadlines of hard real-time tasks are violated. This is done by only allowing to over-allocate a resource if a plan for solving every possible conflict exists and this plan is schedulable under hard real-time constrains. Figure 1.1 illustrates this approach.

4. It is distinguished between resources which can be reassigned with an negligible reallocation time and resources which have to be configured in background by the system software. Resources which are in background reconfigurable need more time to be reassigned between different applications. All resource demands of in background reconfigurable resources – also within the specified limits of the actual profile – require an announcement to the operating system. Between the announcement and the assignment a delay is assumed. The profile specifies a *maximum* delay per background reconfigurable resource. Note that this delay is a worst-case value.

The schedulability and the deadlock freeness of the FRM approach are formally proved in this thesis.

Operating system services can be mapped – like the applications – into profiles and can make use of the FRM. Different profiles model the activation state of the system service: activated, deactivated or limited. The main idea is to block in the deactivated or limited profiles the resources the system service provides when it is fully activated. With this approach the FRM can decide which system services to activate or deactivate depending on the current requirements of the applications. If a service is not required it is deactivated by the FRM and activated timely if an application or other system service needs the service. For this purpose no adaptation of the FRM model is required: from the point of view of the FRM the system services are applications with profiles. With this technique a flexible and adaptive service structure can be build: a self-optimizing real-time operating system. Thus, the resource requirements of the operating system can be minimized during run-time without constricting the functionality of the system software.

To enable engineers to easily use the FRM and respective the profile model, the approach is integrated into the high-level design process of self-optimizing mechatronic systems. A semi-automatic

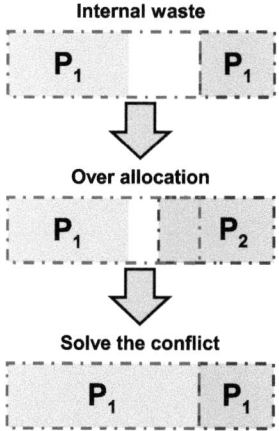

Figure 1.1.: Over allocation.

code generation is presented, which allows a generation of profiles out of hybrid real-time state charts. Hybrid state charts combine continuous models and discrete real-time state charts (e.g. for the reconfiguration model). The application programmer only has to specify a minimum of additional information to generate profiles. For simulation purpose the FRM was not only implemented on top of the operating system DREAMS, but also integrated into MATLAB/SIMULINK. This enables a simulation of an application using the FRM in which the continuous part, including the controller and the plant, of the application is covered.

The benefit of using the FRM approach is presented using case studies of the self-optimizing mechatronic applications and randomized simulations.

1. Summary

2. Introduction

Nowadays the amount of software in technical systems rises extraordinarily, because of the enormous advantages of mechatronic systems. Many modern systems can not operate without software support. Up to 100 micro-controller are used within a modern car, tendency rising. This trend leads to more and more hardware within those systems and therefore is an attractive solution to share it by using real-time operating systems, instead of only employing one software task per micro controller. The reason for the increasing number of micro controllers is the increase of functionality of these software systems. For example, functionality which was in the past realized only by mechanics are now realized as a mechatronic system (e.g. X-By-Wire Technology). Additionally the application area of the systems is changing over time, e.g. due to mobility [Agh02].

Not only in the area of mechatronic systems the functionality and computation power of the systems is increasing; in other embedded systems the trend is also observable. Take the mobile phone as an example: In the beginning the only functionality was to phone, then the functionality increased: short messages support, camera support, music player support, PIM [1] support, internet support and so on. Depending on what a user currently is doing with his mobile phone different demands to the software and hardware of the mobile phone are to be fulfilled. The whole functionality of these systems is not used completely concurrently. Depending of the current use case of the device different software and hardware modules are active and others are inactive.

To cope with the challenges of modern embedded systems (mechatronic or not) an approach is to make these systems more intelligent with multi-agent or self-X techniques like self-optimization or self-organization [VASP09]. Some techniques use nature-inspired approaches. All these techniques help systems to cope with higher dynamics and adapt a system according to environmental changes. In such systems the current situation is observed and the system is optimized. The optimization can be realized from just changing parameters up to changing the system structure itself.

Common with these systems – due to their dynamic behavior – are the changing requirements of the application level software to the underlying middleware and operating system layer. With the increasing functionality of the application level the required functionality of the underlaying layers have to be increased as well to support the applications appropriately [SPT09]. That implies a shift

---

[1] Personal Information Manager

2. Introduction

in the trend of system software from specialized solution to the direction of general purpose system software. Of course on the one hand general purpose system software could serve the wide requests of modern dynamic applications of the embedded and mechatronic field. On the other hand the problem with general purpose system software is its size and thus the resource hunger of this software itself. Classical general purpose system software therefore is too cumbersome. This is specially true in the case of hard real-time systems, where the amount of resources is growing but still more limited than in the case of desktop or high performance computing. To deal with the problem of providing a wide range of functionality in the system software and not to build a dull system software, the layers have to be designed with the same principles as the modern application software: e.g. using self-optimization. This means that the layers have to optimize themselves according to the current application layer requirements and adjust their structure as well [Sch02].

As TANENBAUM stated in [Tan08], the current issue of the standard work in operating system research, the two main functionalities of an operating system are abstraction and resource management. In classical approaches for resource management, applications in real-time systems define worst-case requirements. The classical resource management for real-time systems has to assure that the upper limits from all applications do not exceed the system limits. When these upper limits are only reserved for worst-case resource requirements and do not represent the average case, then this often leads to an internal waste of resources. This means that the applications can only allocate resources within their a priori defined boundaries. The maximum required resources could be needed for example due to complex error handling in case of a failure. In the previously described dynamic scenarios – due to the dynamic behavior – the worst case requirements could be needed only if a special feature or service of the operating system is used. If the feature or service is not used the resource could be put temporarily to other tasks' disposal until the feature is required again. A resource management is required, which on the one hand can detect if applications or system services are not using their reserved resources and on the other hand distribute the unused resources temporarily to other applications' disposal. Thus, it must handle the dynamics of the system. The resource management must be compliant with real-time constrains and provide guaranties [But06].

2.1. Aim of this Thesis

The goal of this thesis is to develop and research concepts for real-time operating systems which are used in the context of self-optimizing systems. As – beside abstraction – resource management is the main purpose of an operating system, in this thesis a Flexible Ressource Manager is developed which overcomes the disadvantages of classical resource management approaches. The following challenging questions summarize the described problems and address the main research directions this thesis is dealing with:

- How to deal with higher dynamics of the application level in the operating system level (resource management, service structure)?
- How to minimize the internal waste due to worst case resource requirements?
- How to get information about the dynamic requirements of applications?
- How to decide which system service can be activated, degraded or deactivated?
- How to distribute freed resources to the application tasks?
- How to guarantee hard real-time constrains while reconfiguring resource assignment?
- How to make guarantees for the QoS (Quality of Service) in dynamic systems?
- How make such a system easy to use for application programmers?

The main contribution of this thesis is the concept of over-allocation under hard real-time constrains, the integration of the resource management into the design process and the deployment of the over-allocation for the creation of a self-optimizing RTOS.

2.2. Classification into the State of the Art

As documented later in Chapter 4_{35} [2] in the state of the art indeed approaches exist to allocate resources dynamically, but most approaches guarantee Quality of Service (QoS) only for soft real-time environments as STANKOVIC and RAJKUMAR describe in [SR04]. A problem is that reassigning resources at run-time leads into changing task sets or tasks with changing periods. The transformation between this different operational modes of applications is called a *mode change* [PB98]. In hard real-time a mode change must not violate real-time constrains of the applications. Resource manager like the Adaptive Resource Management (ARM) Middleware [EJW+03] simplify the problem by assuming zero time reconfiguration between different modes. This approach is not applicable when reconfiguration takes time. FĂRCAŞ stated in [Făr06] that current approaches only support global mode changes; no system allows real-time components to switch modes independently.

In March 2006 BUTTAZZO published in [But06] the current trends in the area of real-time computing for embedded systems. In this article current research demands were attested in the area of reflection, resource awareness as well as information flow from the applications to the operating systems. These are the areas this thesis is engaging in. SCHMIDT in [Sch02] has written a position paper

---
[2]To ease location of references (e.g. to figures, definitions, sections, etc.) references are indexed by the corresponding page number if they are not on the same page.

2. Introduction

about technical challenge in middleware for real-time and embedded systems. He characterized the requirements for new and planned distributed real-time and embedded systems in research as follows:

- Multiple QoS properties must be satisfied in real-time.
- Different levels of service are appropriate under different configurations, environmental conditions and costs.
- The levels of service in one dimension must be coordinated with and/or traded off against the levels of service in other dimensions to meet mission needs.
- The need for autonomous and time critical application behavior necessitates a flexible distributed system substrate that adapts robustly to dynamic changes in mission requirements and environmental conditions.

Thus, the research community attests the questions – presented in the previous section – as well with a high significance.

2.3. Organisation of this Thesis

The remaining content of this thesis is organized as follows:

Part II Foundations and Related Work discusses the foundations of the thesis and the corresponding related work:

Chapter 3 Self-optimization introduces the concept of self-optimization and the terminology/context of the Collaborative Research Center 614 (CRC614), entitled: *Self-Optimizing Concepts and Structures in Mechanical Engineering*. Beside the architecture and the design process demonstrators of the CRC614 are described, which are used later as case studies for the approach of this thesis.

Chapter 4 Real-time Operating Systems and Resource Management discusses the state of the art of real-time operating systems (RTOS) and resource management. Techniques like EDF [3] scheduling are introduced, because the approach of this thesis is using them.

Part III RTOS for self-optimizing mechatronic systems - the concepts contains the main chapters of this thesis:

---
[3]Earliest Deadline First

Chapter 5 The Flexible Resource Manager - Concept describes the main concept of this thesis. It comprises the used formal system model and the description of the developed resource manager. Here, the profile framework, the interface to the resource manager, is introduced and the new resource allocation paradigm *over-allocation* is described. Concluding the chapter, the approach of this thesis is classified according to mode change protocols and the self-optimization concept.

Chapter 6 The Flexible Resource Manager - Analysis proves formally the schedulability of the resource re-assignment and deadlock freeness of the Flexible Resource Manager approach.

Chapter 7 The Flexible Resource Manager - Optimization contains the used optimization techniques inside the resource manager. An event prediction mechanism and algorithms to find a good allocation for the current situation are presented.

Chapter 8 Building a Self-optimizing RTOS applies the Flexible Resource Manager approach to operating system services itself. By this a dynamic RTOS is built, which adapts to the current application requirements e.g. by deactivating unused system services.

Chapter 9 Application Design Flow describes a technique for developer to ease the application of Flexible Resource Manager and its profile interface to their applications. Hybrid state charts, a formal method to describe continuous and discrete behavior in engineering systems, are extended to be used by a semi automatic algorithm to generate multi mode applications which can use the resource manager.

Part IV RTOS for Self-optimizing Mechatronic Systems - Evaluation analyses the Flexible Ressource Manager approach in two chapters by describing application case studies and the appraisal of simulations:

Chapter 10 Case Studies concentrates on example applications and system services using the Flexible Resource Manager approach. The chapter clarifies the use of the profile interface and how applications can be modeled in a multi mode manner. In addition an extension of the Flexible Resource Manager approach is presented, which transfuses the stress behavior (acute stress response) of human beings to the resource management.

Chapter 11 Simulation investigates the benefit of the Flexible Resource Manager while executing multiple applications on top of it. For this purpose a Matlab/Simulink based simulator of the Flexible Resource Manager is used. First an example is presented where concrete applications share resources via the Flexible Resource Manager. Second the results of the simulation of multiple randomly generated application sets executed in top of the Flexible Resource Manager

2. Introduction

are discussed. With this simulation different Flexible Resource Manager characteristics are evaluated against each other.

Part V Outlook and Conclusion gives a summary and outlook for this thesis:

Chapter 12 Conclusion and Outlook concentrates the main contribution of this thesis and gives an outlook on some ideas, where research of this thesis could be deepened.

2.4. Overview of Publications of the Author Related to this Thesis

As the work of this thesis is done within the Collaborative Research Center 614 in the subproject C2 named '*RTOS for self-optimizing applications*', part of the work of this thesis was previously published on conferences or workshops:

The main concept of the Flexible Resource Manger had been published in the proceedings of the of *IFIP Working Conference on Distributed and Parallel Embedded Systems (DIPES'04)* [OB04].

Section 6.1_{63}, in which the schedulability of resource reassignment is formally proven, is mainly based on an article presented at the *DASMOD Workshop on Formal Verification of Adaptive Systems* in 2007 [LO07].

The concept of event prediction presented in Section 7.1_{82}, the look-ahead optimization of Section 12.3_{149} and the case study of the Active Suspension System of Section 10.1_{121} were published in the *Proceedings of the 7th International Heinz Nixdorf Sysmposium: Self-optimizing Mechatronic Systems* in 2008 [OZK08].

The concept of SORTOS from 8_{91} was published in the proceedings of the *5th ACM international conference on Embedded software (EMSOFT'2005)* [OBG05]. The corresponding case study presented in Section 8.4_{101} was presented at the *International Embedded Systems Symposium 2005* [GOP05].

Chapter 9_{107} had been taken from a publication at the *4th ACM International Conference on Embedded Software (EMSOFT'2004)* [BGGO04].

The application of the FRM for Acute Stress Response in Resource Management presented in Section 10.3_{124} is based on an article published in the *Proceedings of the IFIP Conference on Biologically Inspired Cooperative Computing* in 2006 [GMM$^+$06].

Part II.

Foundations and Related Work

3. Self-optimization

The next generation of advanced mechatronic systems is expected to behave more intelligently than today's systems. They adjust their goals and behavior according to changes of the environment or system and build communities of autonomous agents. The agents exploit local and global networking to enhance their functionality (cf. [Wir04]). Thus, such mechatronic systems will include complex real-time reconfiguration of the underlying software and hardware as well as complex real-time coordination to adjust their behavior to the changing system goals leading to self-optimization (os self-adaptation) [SKB98, MGPK99, OGT+99, FGK+04, ADG+08]. Thus, self-optimization is a promising approach to build advanced intelligent mechatronic systems.

In this chapter the self-optimizing approach is explained in the context of the Collaborative Research Center 614 [1] . This is the context, in which this thesis is originated. In 3.1 the Collaborative Research Center is briefly introduced and the concept and terms of self-optimization are defined (3.2_{16} and 3.3_{17}). After this the main concepts of designing and building self-optimizing mechatronic systems are presented: The architecture 3.4_{17}, a dependability concept 3.5_{19}, a platform for self-optimizing applications 3.6_{20} and the design process 3.7_{22}. After that demonstrators, which are used later in this thesis as case studies, are introduced in 3.8_{22}.

3.1. Collaborative Research Center 614

The Collaborative Research Center 614 (CRC 614) *Self-Optimizing Concepts and Structures in Mechanical Engineering* uses self-optimization as the central approach, as the title denotes. The scenario of the CRC 614 are the mechatronic systems of tomorrow. These systems will be a configuration of system elements with inherent intelligence. The behavior of the complete system is influenced by communication and cooperation of the intelligent system elements. From the information technology point of view this is a system of cooperating agents. The agents internally and the cooperation archetype of the agents use the concept of self-optimization. The CRC 614 defines self-optimization [GFS06, FGK+04, ADG+08] as described in the following section.

---
[1]The presented work in this chapter is derived from the researches of the CRC 614 and not only from the author of this thesis.

3.2. Definition of Self-Optimization

In allusion to the definition in the DIN 19226 norm [DIN02a], the definition of self-optimization uses the concept of system, which is established by elements. Elements themselves can be systems. The concept of system is defined in a flexible way to support applicability to different systems and their system boundaries.

Definition 1. Self-optimization *takes place in a system if and only if the following three activities are recurringly executed through collaboration of the elements of the system:*

1. *Analysis of the current situation*
2. *Determination of the system objectives*
3. *Adaptation of the system behavior*

Essential for self-optimization is that system objectives are adjusted and committed autonomously and situationally by the system. A system in which only the first and third activities take place contains no self-optimization. The three activities comprise the following details:

- **Analysis of the current situation**: The first activity considers the current situation, which enfolds the state of the system as well as the possible observations the system makes of its environment. Observations can also be made indirectly through communication with other systems. The state of the system furthermore can contain previously stored observations. An essential aspect of this analysis is examining how much the pursued system objectives are fulfilled.

- **Determination of the system objectives**: In the second activity new objectives for the system can be emerged through selection, adaption or generation. Selection means choosing one alternative from a predefined discrete finite set of possible objectives. In contrast, an adaption of objectives describes a gradual modification of existing objectives. Generation of objectives means the creation of new objectives independently of the existing ones.

- **Adaptation of the system behavior**: The adjustment of the system behavior, because of previous modification of the system objectives, is called *behavior adaptation*. Behavior adaptation is achieved by changing the structure or parameters of a respectively lower hierarchical layer. In this third activity of the self-optimizing process the concluding reaction of the self-optimizing cycle through adaptation of the system behavior is described. The individual adaptation cases may be extremely diverse, depending on which level of the mechatronic system the action takes place. The domain, in which the adaptation takes place also plays an essential role.

Optimization, in the sense of a concrete optimization algorithm, can take place within the second activity of the self-optimizing process, when determining the system objectives, and within the third activity, when determining the preferable adaptation regarding to the selected system objectives. Between the activities only a causal dependency in form of the necessary information flow is required. The outcomes of the analysis of the current situation build the basis of the determination of the system objectives. On the other hand the adaption of the system behavior depends on the determinate system objectives. There exists also a natural cause-effect relationship between the realized adaption and the resulting observed current situation.

3.3. Objectives and System of Objectives

The intention of self-optimization is to enable a system to behave according to its system of objectives. The system of objectives is in general a set of objectives, which are related to each other. A system of objectives can be realized as an objective vector or, if an order exist, an objective hierarchy. Complex connections can be described as an objective graph.

Objectives describe the demanded, wanted or to be avoided behavior of the system. Objectives are classified as external, inherent or internal ones.

3.4. Architecture of the Information Processing of Self-Optimizing Systems

As advanced mechatronic systems usually consist of a complex network of concurrently running components which are also called (software) agents, a general architectural model of its components the so-called Operator-Controller Module (OCM) [HOG04] has been developed in the CRC 614. Within a single autonomous mechatronic system, a hierarchy of OCMs is employed to define the strictly hierarchical architecture. In contrast, at the top level the OCMs are free to connect to their peers to establish the required coordination.

The OCM suggests the following internal structuring, which is illustrated in Figure 3.1_{18}:

1. On the lowest level of the OCM, there is the *controller*, which realizes the currently active control strategy, processes measurements and produces the control signals.

2. The *reflective operator*, in which monitoring and controlling routines are executed, monitors the controller.

3. The *cognitive operator* is trying to improve the behavior of the OCM in soft real-time.

3. Self-optimization

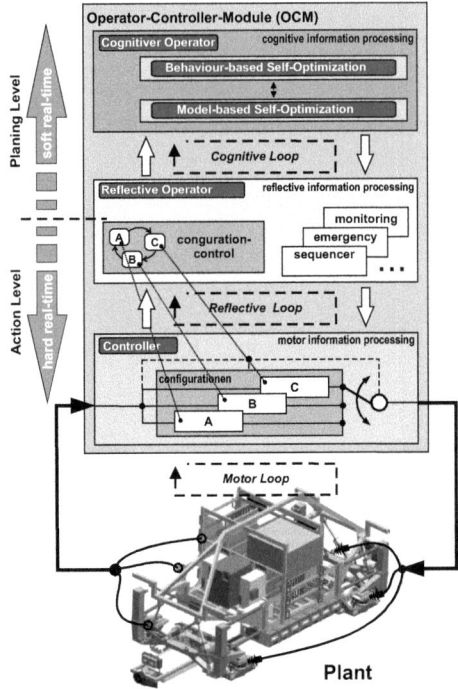

Figure 3.1.: Structure of an Operator-Controller Module (OCM).

While the proposed OCM architecture is mainly driven by the requirements for self-optimizing mechatronic behavior, it also shows some similarities with several layered architectures proposed in literature. [Her04] suggests that a two-level architecture with a low-level execution and a higher-level control layer represents a general pattern presented in natural as well as artificial organic systems. A related practical approach explained in [SMS05] is the Observer/Controller architecture for Organic Computing systems. Similar to the OCM, it is inspired in the *brain stem* as low level structures which reacts to sensory inputs and the *limbic system* as a high-level structure which observes and manipulates the first one. In contrast to this work, the OCM also supports higher cognitive behavior which matches the planning layer of the Turing Machines [Fer92] (autonomous agents with attitudes). Additionally, the OCM tries to reach the goal of a general model for autonomous cognitive agents as stated in [VD98], which explains the action selection paradigm of mind for conscious software agents

3.5. Multi-stage Dependability Concept

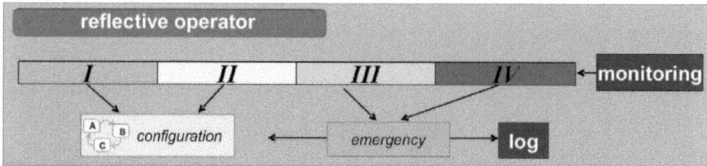

Figure 3.2.: Monitoring Concept for self-optimizing Systems.

and how the most relevant behavior/action is selected and executed.

3.5. Multi-stage Dependability Concept

The following concept was developed in order to protect OCMs systematically against hazards or faults [GMM+06]. These hazards or faults might result from their cognitive self-optimizing behavior.

The monitoring is integrated in the reflectoring operator of the OCM. The monitoring concept is a guideline, when and how self-optimization is reasonable to use. Furthermore it describes which emergency categories should be supported and when a switching between them should be initiated to avoid major consequences (cf. Fig. 3.2). The monitoring concept distinguishes four different emergency categories:

I   The system operates regularly and uses the self-optimization for the major system objectives; e.g. comfort and energy efficiency if useful.

II A possible threat has been detected and the self-optimization is not only used to optimize the behavior but also to reach system states, which are considered to be safer than the current one.

III A hazard, that endangers the system, has been detected. Fast and robust countermeasures, like a reflex, are performed in the reflective operator in hard real-time in order to reach a safer state (I or II). Depending on the specific OCM, configurations where the cognitive reactions run in the background may still be employed, configurations with additional functionality may be employed, or only robust configurations without self-optimization are used.

IV The system is no longer under control; the system must be immediately stopped or a minimal safe-operational mode must be warranted to minimize damage. In rare cases, cognitive reactions in the OCM may be employed in order to rescue the system if no fail-safe or minimal fail-operational behavior is possible.

3.6. Platform for Self-Optimizing Applications

As self-optimizing systems are dynamic at run-time due to reconfiguration they have special demands at the underlying hardware/software platform. The platform has to deal with the changing resource requirements of the self-optimizing applications and must support reconfiguration under hard real-time constrains. Designing this platform statically would lead to waste of resources as not all services/features are required all the time by the applications, as described in the introduction in Chapter 2_7. Thus, the platform itself reconfigures itself at run-time to adapt to the actual requirements and frees resources of services/features which are not required. The Flexible Resource Manger of this thesis plays a fundamental role in this platform.

In the proposed approach of the CRC 614 dynamic reconfiguration is provided by a combination of dynamically reconfigurable hardware and a reconfigurable real-time operating system (RTOS). While the proposed hardware platform offers the fundamental mechanisms that are required to execute arbitrary software and to exchange hardware modules at run-time, the RTOS delivers an interface to the middleware **I**ntegration **P**latform for **N**etworked **M**echatronic **A**pplications (IPANEMA) [Hon98, GO03] and the Flexible Resource Manager, which is part of the RTOS, optimizes the resource assignment in general and thus, decides whether a task is executed in software, in hardware, or in a combination of both.

Software Environment

The run-time platform IPANEMA allows execution of continuous models based on ODE (Ordinary Differential Equations) as well as of discrete systems in real-time. Platform-independent code generation of executable models becomes possible when model, solver, and operating system are separated.

The Real-time Operating System library **D**istributed **R**eal-time **E**xtensible **A**pplication **M**anagement **S**ystem (DREAMS) (comp. Section 8.1_{92}) is used, which contains the *Flexible Resource Management* (FRM) framework of this thesis. The FRM provides a self-optimizing resource allocation infrastructure for the target scenario.

A core component of the proposed architecture is the *Run-time Reconfiguration Manager* (RTR-Manager) [GVPR04], providing the interface to the reconfigurable hardware. Therefore, it offers services for controlling and monitoring of the hardware configuration and supports the dynamic partial reconfiguration of hardware modules.

3.6. Platform for Self-Optimizing Applications

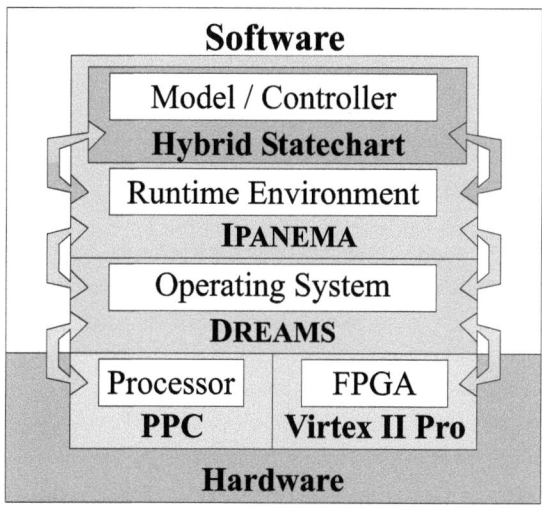

Figure 3.3.: Platform for self-optimizing systems - overview.

Hardware Environment

When principles of self-optimization refer to the topology and structure of microelectronic systems, a reconfigurability of the system architecture or of dedicated system components is required. In this context reconfigurability means the possibility to change the functionality or interconnection of hardware modules in microelectronic systems before and during operation. In the CRC 614 state of the art Field Programmable Gate Arrays (FPGAs) are used, which facilitate System on Programmable Chip (SoPC) designs with a complexity of more than a million logic gates and several hundred kBytes of internal SRAM memory. Clock rates of applications on modern FPGAs approach several hundred MHz increasing the chip-computational power above 10^4 MOPS (million operations per second) at a power consumption of a few watts.

Today's FPGAs combine the flexibility of programmable logic and the high performance of embedded processor cores or other hard-macros. The motivation behind this trend stems from performance requirements and silicon efficiency. Soft-cores targeting larger FPGAs sometimes result in unacceptable performance limitations due to low-clock frequency. In comparison to that an embedded processor hard-macro can run in a speed range comparable to ASIC-based counterparts. For the implementation in the CRC 614 scenario, a Xilinx Virtex-II Pro FPGAs is used. The Virtex-II Pro is a SoPC architecture, which integrates dynamically reconfigurable hardware blocks and up to four embedded PowerPC processors. The modular Rapid Prototyping System RAPTOR2000 [KPR02] integrates these SoPCs into mechatronic systems together with additional components like memory and peripherals.

3.7. Design of Self-optimizing Systems

To enable self-optimizing systems to be developed, a concept for the development process was proposed within the CRC 614. This concept helps to integrate self-optimizing concepts (e.g. system of objectives) into the development of mechatronic systems [Sch06], beginning from the early development phases (conception) [GKP08] up to the operation phase. Partial models are used to describe the domain specific principle solutions [GFDK08]. The solutions are then refined in the domain specific manner and thereafter integrated to a detailed overall solution. To ease the conception on system level, predefined solutions can be selected by use of a morphological analysis [GZF$^+$07]. To increase dependability, classical and novel methods are used in every development phase.

Software Development

For the development of software components for self-optimizing systems – especially for the development of OCMs – MECHATRONIC UML [BGT05, GHH$^+$08] was developed, which is based on UML 2.0. MECHATRONIC UML allows to model structure and behavior of mechatronic systems and the interaction between them. Real-time state-charts are used to model hard real-time behavior. It depicts a complete development method from modeling over formal verification up to code generation [GTB$^+$03, GBSO04]. For the integration of continues control algorithms, hybrid state charts can be used. In hybrid state charts the continues behavior is embedded in each discrete state. The CASE tool Fujaba [2] and the CAE tool CAMeL-View [3] support the development method.

3.8. Demonstrators of the Collaborative Research Center 614

As a concrete example in the CRC 614 the Paderborn-based RailCab research project [4] is used. The modular railway system combines sophisticated undercarriages with the advantage of new actu-

---

[2] http://www.fujaba.de
[3] http://www.ixtronics.com/ix_hist/English/CAMeLView.htm
[4] http://www-nbp.upb.de/en

3.8. Demonstrators of the Collaborative Research Center 614

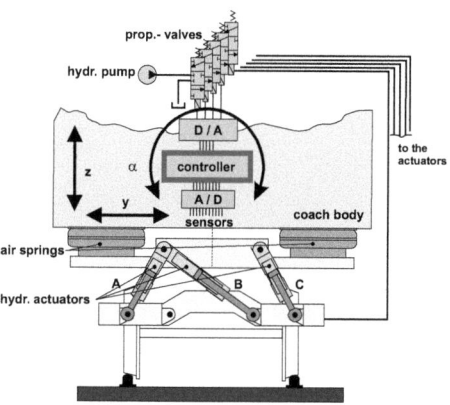

Figure 3.4.: Active Suspension System

ation techniques as employed in the Transrapid [5] to increase passenger comfort, enabling efficient transportation at a high average speed, and (re)using of the existing railway tracks. The autonomous RailCab shuttles are powered by a double loaded linear drive [BSSZ05]. Different subcomponents have been implemented as isolated hardware-in-the-loop breadboard constructions. The ones which are used as a case study (comp. Chapter 10_{121}) for the Flexible Resource Manager are now described. The level of detail for the description of each demonstrator is chosen on the base of the case studies. The details are important to understand how this applications can be modeled using the Flexible Ressource Manager.

3.8.1. Active Suspension System

The main task of the active suspension system of the railcab [VT08] is to improve the riding comfort for the passengers of the railcab by reducing the influences of track excitations to the coach body. Therefore, in the suspension system passive dampers are left out. The necessary damping forces are calculated depending on the movement of the coach body and induced by an active displacement of the spring bases by means of hydraulic cylinders. The basic control strategy uses the relative movement between the chassis and the coach body to emulate the function of passive dampers for low frequencies. Additionally, the comfort can be increased using the absolute movement of the coach body that is gained from acceleration sensors. This kind of control is known as *skyhook* [LG99]. If

---
[5] http://www.transrapid.de/en

3. Self-optimization

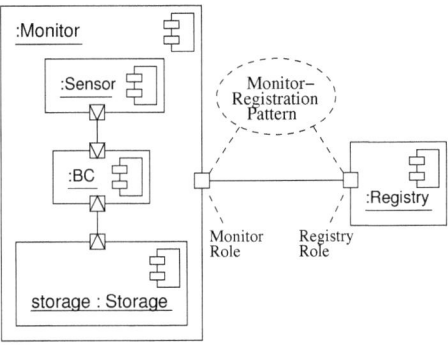

Figure 3.5.: Structure of the overall system

the topology of the track is available in advance exactly, the comfort can be improved even more by means of a feed forward disturbance compensation [TMV06]. However, in this case the reference data about the track characteristics have to be processed and adjusted individually to each vehicle. Thus, multiple feedback controllers are to be applied with different capabilities in matters of safety and comfort.

The main objective of the OCM in the active suspension system is to achieve the comfort with a minimum amount of energy. Depending on the actual situation the active suspension system activates and deactivates the additional control strategies described above. On a very smooth track the complex control algorithms like skyhook and disturbance compensation are not necessary. Here the simple control of the relative movement between the chassis and the coach body achieves nearly the same quality while requiring fewer resources on the information processing level (e.g. CPU utilization or memory). Hence, with high probability the application for the control of the active suspension system requires little resources on smooth track sections. On the other hand on rough track sections the skyhook control and the disturbance compensation are probably activated to keep up a high degree of comfort. The needed track information are stored at the track, therefore known in advance and useable for planning.

Model of the Active Suspension System Demonstrator

The demonstrator of the active suspension system was modeled using design methods as recommended in the scope of the CRC 614. Thus, a real-time state chart model of the system exists. Figure 3.5 depicts the structure of the overall system, consisting of the registry and the agent's monitor com-

3.8. Demonstrators of the Collaborative Research Center 614

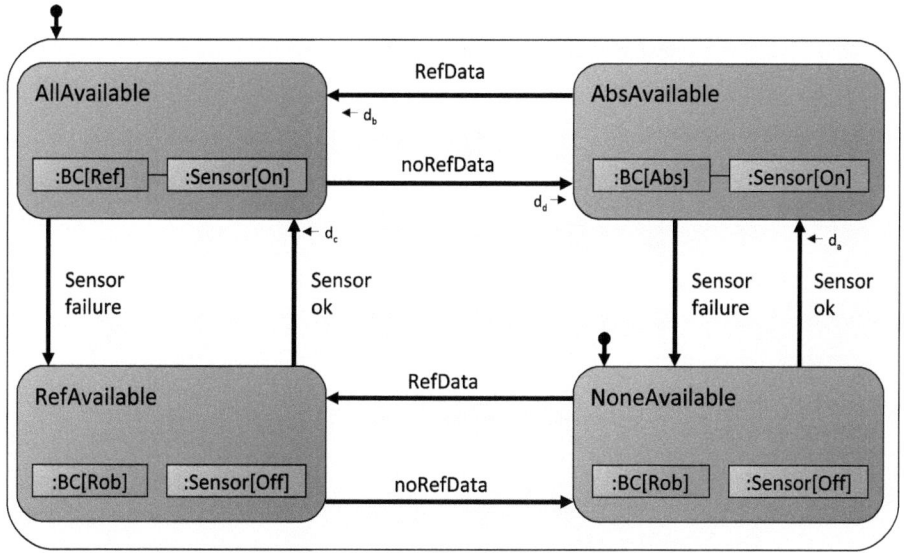

Figure 3.6.: Simplified state chart of the active suspension system.

ponent, which embeds a sensor, a storage, and the Body Control (BC). The sensor delivers the $\ddot{z}_{abs}$ signal (absolute movement), in the storage the reference curve is stored and the BC component is responsible for the chassis control. The monitor's task is to coordinate the BC component dependent on the available signals from the sensor and storage. In the simplified model three different controlling strategies are distinguished inside the controlling component body control (BC):

Reference In this mode complex control including skyhook and disturbance compensation is used. Thus, reference, relative and absolute data are required.

Absolute In this mode the skyhook mode is active, no disturbance compensation is used. Relative and absolute data are required.

Relative In this mode only the basic control strategy is used, only the relative data is required.

Additionally, a passive mode in which the coach body is not active sprung is feasible. In this mode only the damping of the vehicle's structure is used. This mode is applicable in case of complete sensor

3. Self-optimization

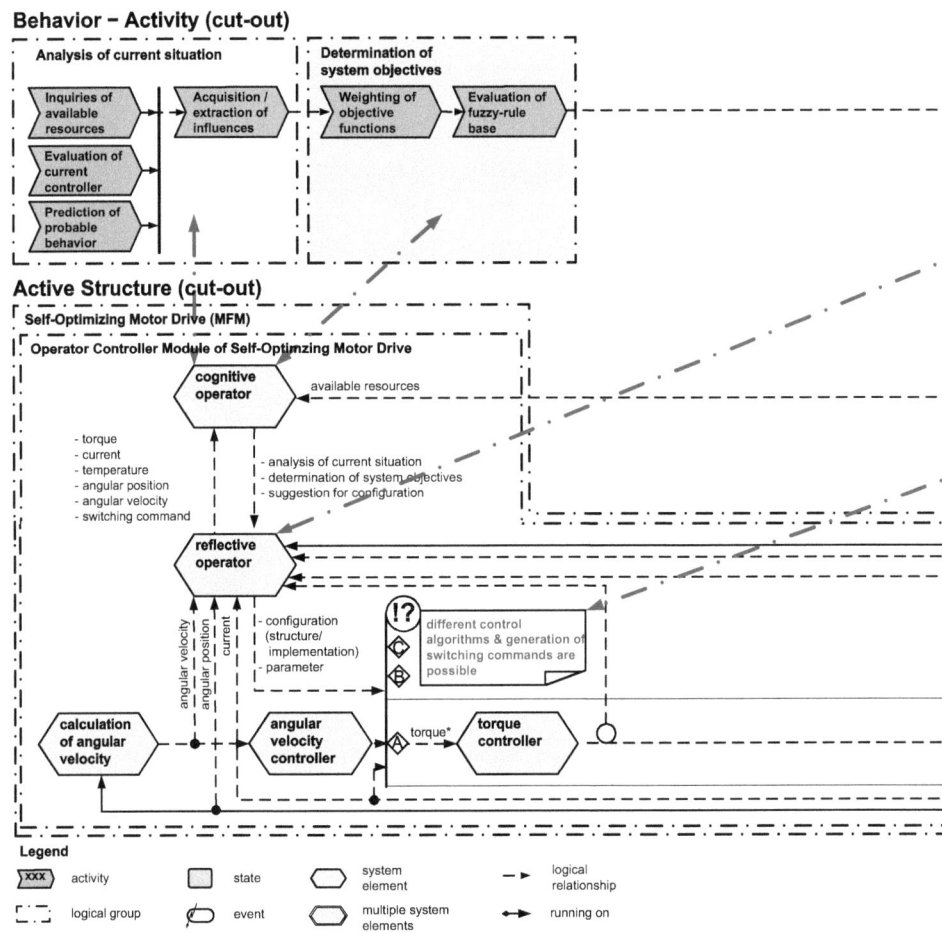

Figure 3.7.: behavior, activities and states of the self-optimizing drive control OCM

3.8. Demonstrators of the Collaborative Research Center 614

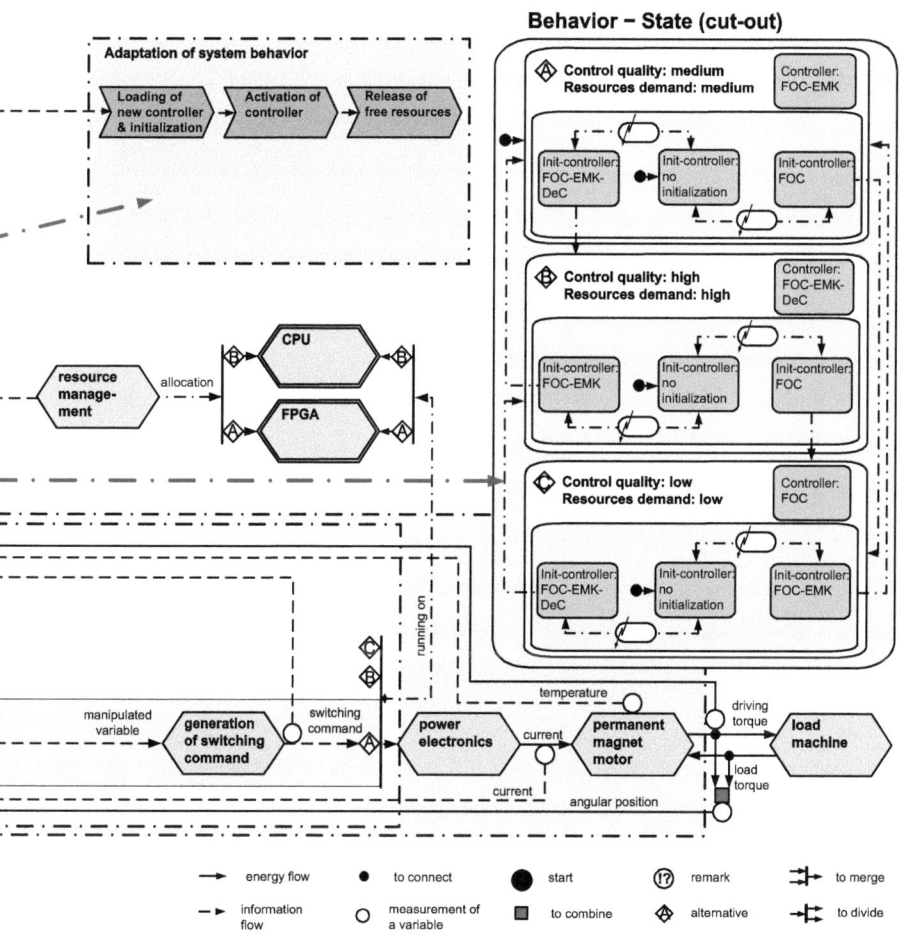

3. Self-optimization

failure as a fall-back strategy. However, for simplicity this mode is not considered in the statechart model.

The behavior of the monitor is specified by the real-time statechart from Figure 3.6_{25}. For simplicity only a simplified version of the statechart is presented. For example reconfiguration triggered by the cognitive operator is not included. Only sensor failures are modeled. The model consists of four states, representing which of the two signals (absolute and reference) are available or not. Transitions are time consuming and associated with a minimum and a maximum duration interval d. In order to coordinate the monitor and the body control, the configurations of the subordinated components are embedded into the statechart that describes the monitor's behavior. Each discrete state of the monitor is associated with a configuration of the embedded components, that specifies which components and connections are required and in which discrete state the embedded components have to reside. For example, a transition from state AllAvailable to AbsAvailable implies a state change of BC from mode Reference to Absolute. A detailed description of the design and the concept for hybrid statecharts and hybrid components can be found in [GBSO04, BGO04].

3.8.2. Self-optimizing Drive Control

The self-optimizing drive control is an OCM which controls an electric motor. The goal of the OCM can be to hold a specific torsional or number of revolutions at different load conditions.

In the demonstrator, build in the CRC 614, the load is generated by another electric motor with standard control algorithms and hardware. The OCM has to compensate this load. With this breadboard construction different load profiles can be simulated. This load profiles can be loaded torsional respectively the number of revolutions each with chronological alteration.

The special ability of the self-optimizing process inside the OCM of this demonstrator is the adaptation to different resource specifications (memory, cpu-time, space on FPGA) which are provided by the resource management of the operating system. Depending on the current situation (e.g. load) different qualities can be reached with external resource specification. The cognitive operator of this OCM is responsible for selecting the appropriate control strategy; the decision is taken on the base of the system of objectives. The objectives for the decision take the current situation and the external resource specification into account. Thus, the actual concrete resource requirements depend on the decisions of the cognitive operator. Additionally, the OCM can facilitate the use of different resource types. Some parts of the control algorithm can be executed not only in CPU but also as a hardware alternative inside the FPGA.

The OCM can run in two different scenarios:

Minimizing the resources: The OCM gets a specified resource bound defined from the resource management of the system and tries to select the controller with the lowest resource requirements in which the system operates still safe. This mode is good for constant load situations, when no big control effort is required to control the system. The OCM can report the current quality to the resource management according to the quality of control. Thus, the resource manager, as an superior instance, is the main instance of decision.

Maximizing quality of control: In this mode also the OCM gets a specified resource bound, but it tries to maximize the quality of control under this specific resource boundary. If the best quality of control can be reached with a controller with lower resource requirements this one is selected and unused resources can be assigned to other applications by the resource manager.

Depending on this two modes the objectives in the system of objectives are weighted different.

In Figure 3.7_{26} a cut-out of the model of the demonstrator is presented [GKLS07]. The figure shows the behavior of the self-optimizing activities, the behavior in form of states of the controller and the structure of the hardware and software components, which are involved.

The OCM is executed on a RAPTOR2000 system with a Virtex-II FPGA and a Virtex-II-Pro FPGA containing a PowerPC processor.

3.8.3. Operating Point Assignment

The operating point assignment is a part of the motion control inside the driving module of the railcab.

Figure 3.8_{30} shows the structure of the driving module of the linear motor of the railway system. The driving module consists of doubly fed linear drive with magnetic active coils at the track and at the vehicle. The magnetic fields of the coils are supported by the electrical currents, which are predetermined with their frequency by the operating point assignment. The driving module has two purposes: Accelerating and braking the Railcab and transferring energy from the track to the railcab to charge its battery. Thence, the operating point assignment of the linear drive is pivotal for the proper work of the whole vehicle. Without a suitable operating point assignment, a safe and dependable work of the railway system is not possible.

A simple operating point assignment can be handled by a fully powered primary at the track. This fixed operation point leads to an inefficient operation of the system. To improve this efficiency the operating point assignment can be done by a simple efficiency-optimal algorithm outlined in [Pot05]. The concept of self-optimizing in mechatronic systems allows a more powerful operating point assignment [WSD+08]. This self-optimizing operating point assignment enables the system to self-adapt to the system objectives as a response to changes in the surrounding of the system. In case of a low charge state at the energy storage system in the vehicle, the losses in the vehicle

3. Self-optimization

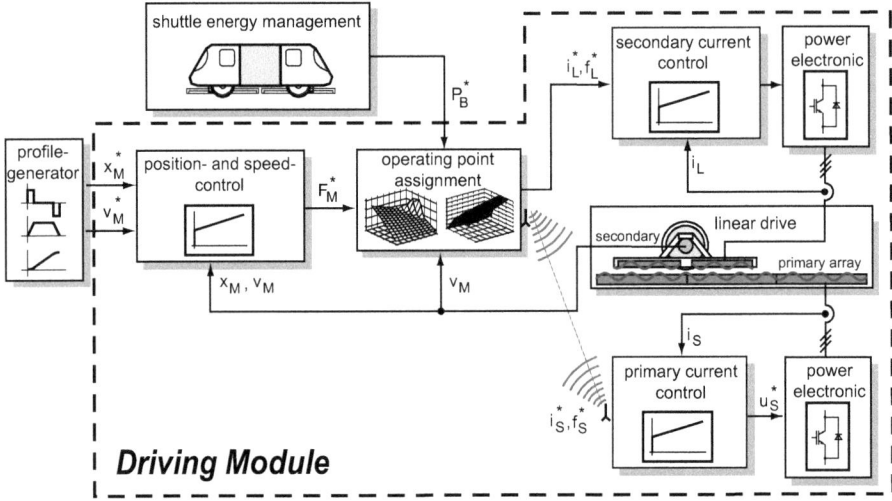

Figure 3.8.: Structure of the Driving Module with operating point assignment.

become more important than the efficiency of the whole system. Otherwise, the efficiency of the whole system can be maximized while the power transfer is not in the focus of the operating point assignment. Moreover, the importance of the power transfer to the vehicle depends on the expected consumption and distance profile of the track.

In Figure 3.9_{31} a simplified statechart is presented, which depicts the parallel processing of the different layers in the cognitive and reflective operator as well as the controller inside the OCM of the operating point assignment. The states have the following meaning: The controller has to support the motion *Control* of the vehicle at all circumstances. The reflective operator at first has to support the critical tasks of *Analyzing* the advisability of the optimized set points for the controller. In the parallel *Adjust* state, the reflective operator remains in the *Normal* state and provides optimized set points to the controller as long as suitable set points where available. Otherwise, in case of inappropriate set points, which can be the result of an unexpected thrust demand or quick changing parameters of the motor, the *Adjust* state of the reflective operator will switch over to the *Emergency* state. In parallel, the *Parameter Estimation* state is required for parameter estimation of the motor parameters to enable the cognitive operator to make a suitable optimization. In the cognitive operator of the OCM suitable objectives for the next optimization cycle are elected in the *Pre-Adjust* state. At the *Optimization*

3.9. Requirements of Self-Optimizing Applications

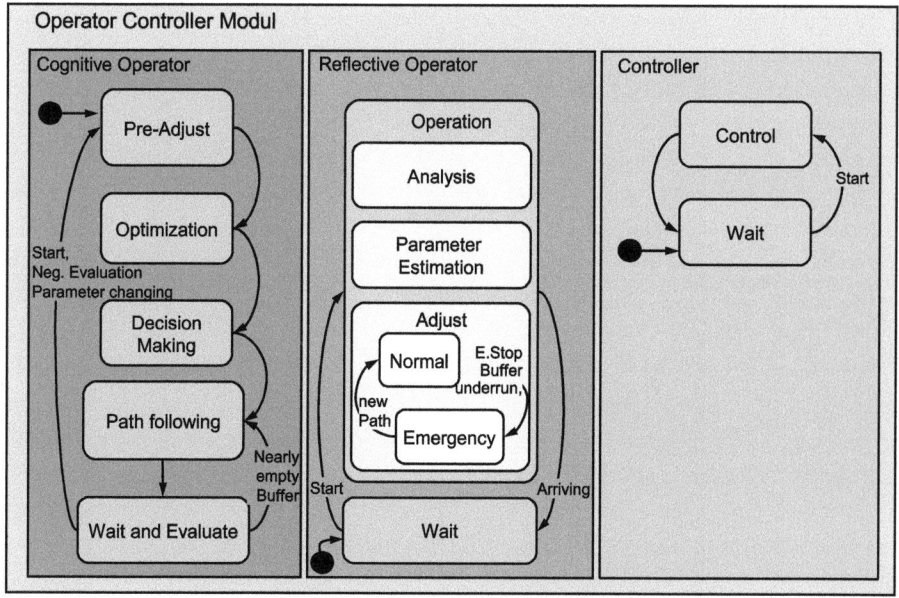

Figure 3.9.: States of the Operating Point Assignment OCM.

state, the multi objective optimization is done and afterwards the pareto point selection follows in the *Decision Making* state. The selected operating point for a discrete time is then employed in the *Path Following* state to calculate the selected operating point for the next few seconds of operation. This calculated path will be send to the reflective operator and a review of the calculated optimization results in the *Wait and Evaluate* state is used to decide whether a new optimization cycle is required or whether it is sufficient to continue the path jumping to the *Path Following* state.

3.9. Requirements of Self-Optimizing Applications

Self-optimizing applications have a highly dynamic behavior due to the self-optimization process. This causes dynamic resource requirements on the different levels of the OCM structure. First, look at the level of the cognitive operator: due to the self-optimizing character, the OCM is analyzing permanently the current situation, determining the system objectives and adapting the system behavior accordingly. Thus, a change of the current situation triggers the dynamic behavior of the applications.

3. Self-optimization

If the current situation does not change over a longer period of time, the resource requirements for the self-optimization process inside the cognitive operator can decrease. They decrease whenever the system objectives for the situation are identified and the adaptation of the system behavior to the situation is completed. At the time when the situation changes the resource requirements of the self-optimizing process in the cognitive operator and in the reflective operator may increase. Then again the situation has to be analyzed, goals have to be aligned and the adaptation of the behavior can lead into an exchange/reconfiguration of the algorithm used in the controller part of the OCM. So on the level of the controller itself this change leads to dynamic resource requirements, as, depending on the current situation, different control algorithms are applicable. Thus, most self-optimizing applications are multi mode applications, which dynamically change their resource requirements during run-time.

According to the real-time aspect self-optimizing applications have different levels of real-time requirements. The architecture definition of the OCM splits a self-optimizing mechatronic system into hard and soft real-time tasks. The reflective operator and the controller belong to the hard real-time domain. They are controlling the plant directly and missing deadlines can have catastrophic consequences. The cognitive operator belongs to the soft real-time domain. It is only responsible for optimizations, but not for the dependability. This also allows using algorithms in the cognitive operator, which cannot guarantee to find an optimized solution for the current situation in time. For example, if the situation changes before the cognitive operator finishes the self-optimization process, the calculations may be unfeasible, but this has no impact on the dependability of the system.

The hard real-time control in mechatronic systems has special requirements according to the communication with the sensors and actuators. For the control algorithm it is important that the interval between the measurements of one sensor is constant. Thus, a small or even no jitter is required. The same is true for setting the output values to the actuator. In the presented platform for self-optimizing systems (comp. Section 3.6_{20}) the buffer registers in the hardware make sure that the sensors are readout and new actuator values are set at the specific points of time with a constant interval. Controllers implemented on the CPU can access the sensor data at an arbitrary point of time and get the value of the sensors of the last point of time the hardware has read out the sensor. According to this the actuator is accessed; new values written to the hardware are transferred to the real actuator at the next specific point of time. This is considered in the control algorithms and allows an arbitrary execution of the controller between two sensors readings respectively sensor readings and a write to the actuators.

As modern mechatronic systems exist out of multiple controllers and sensor data is not only evaluated locally, these systems have also hard real-time requirements according to the communication. Self-optimizing systems, compared to classical mechatronic systems, have additional communication demands, due to communication between different OCMs. Depending on the level of communication (cognitive operator, reflective operator or controller) different real-time requirements are needed.

3.9.1. Summarized Requirements to the System Software

From the previous descriptions in this chapter the requirements of self-optimizing applications to the system software can be summarized to the following accentuated points:

- Multi mode support
- Hard and soft real-time support
- Dynamic resource management support
- Hard real-time communication support

Combining these requirements with the overall requirement to build an efficient real-time operating system the conclusion is to build a *self-optimizing real-time operating system*, which adapts itself to the dynamic concrete application requirements during run-time.

3.10. Chapter Conclusion

The self-optimization concept, introduced in this chapter, is a promising approach to build modern intelligent mechatronic systems with increased functionality for multiple operational areas. The presented demonstrators of the CRC 614 denote the benefit of the approach and are used in Chapter 10_{121} to demonstrated how applications can use the Flexible Resource Manager of this thesis. In the last section the requirements of self-optimizing applications were discussed. The high dynamics in resource requirements of the self-optimizing applications punctuate the demand to a special operating system infrastructure, which can handle these demands efficiently and support the applications by their self-optimization process. Especially a resource manager is needed, which can handle the dynamics under hard real-time constrains and reconfigure the operating system service to the only required quality of service.

3. Self-optimization

4. Real-time Operating Systems and Resource Management

Real-time operating systems afford assistance for scheduling, resource management, synchronization, communication, and precise timing behavior as well as support for I/O. Like classical operating systems for desktop systems, the class of real-time operating systems builds a hardware abstraction from application's point of view.

In the past real-time operating systems for special application areas were considered in research first, afterwards often architectures for universal real-time operating systems were investigated. A widespread activity in research of real-time operating systems afford a multitude of experimental real-time operating systems. Miscellaneous real-time concepts have been examined with this operating systems. Some of those operating systems are: ARTS [TM89], DREAMS [Dit00], HARTOS [KKS89], MARS [KDK+89], MMLite [HF98], OS-Kit [FBB+97], PURE [BGP+99], Pebble [GSB+99], RT-Mach [TNR90], Rialto [JMF+96] or SPRING [SRN+99].

The use of real-time operating systems in embedded systems has multiple advantages:

- The developer can concentrate himself on the implementation process of the system's functionality on the essentials. The operating system abstracts from the hardware and allows the developer a simplified access to the hardware through an *Application Programming Interface* (API). Hereby, the duration of the development process until the commercial launch of the product is decreased drastically.

- An operating system can increase the dependability of the system, especially if multiple functions/applications are realized on the same processor. The operating system in this case can assure a secure separation among the applications, if a corresponding hardware support is present. So, for example, a faulty application has no effect on other components, which are executed on the same controller.

In the market a huge number of real-time operating systems exists, which were developed for different domains respectively exist in different characteristics. Modifications of non real-time operating systems exist as well as independent developed real-time operating systems. Operating systems like

4. Real-time Operating Systems and Resource Management

ELinOS [SYS09a], RTAI [Yag01] or LynxOS [1] are modifications of the OS linux. Independent developed commercial RTOS are OSE[Str09], PikeOS [SYS09b], QNX [Sys08] or VxWorks [Sys09c].

In the following, first a classification scheme for real-time operating systems is presented and then RTOS approaches of different categories are discussed in Section 4.1. After that, in Section 4.2_{40} scheduling algorithms are presented, which are later in this thesis used by the FRM approach. Standards in the field of real-time operating systems are discussed in Section 4.3_{43}

4.1. RTOS Classification

A good overview paper about real-time operating systems was written by STANKOVIC and RAJKUMAR in 2004 [SR04]. They classify real-time operating systems in the following overlapping categories / paradigms: Real-time Extensions for Commercial Operating Systems, Component-based Real-Time Operating Systems, QoS-based Real-Time Operating Systems, Reflective Operating Systems and Resource Kernels. In the following subsections the categories are described and important candidates are presented:

4.1.1. Real-time Extensions for Commercial Operating Systems

A common approach is to extend existing non-real-time operating systems to make them real-time capable. To reach this goal, different methods are applied. One possibility is to build an independent, new operating system with real-time functionality, which has a compatible interface to the existing operating system. LynxOS [2] is an example of this approach.

Another method is to implement a dual operating system kernel. Here the not real-time capable operating system is executed as idle task on top of a small real-time kernel. The real-time kernel handles the hardware access, thus interrupts are intercepted by the real-time kernel. A slim real-time scheduler takes care of the real-time tasks within the real-time kernel. RTAI [Yag01] is using this approach.

A third method is to modify the existing non real-time capable operating system itself. In this approach the main focus is to modify the time response to accomplish deterministic response times of the operating systems and the adaption of the scheduler to a real-time one. RT-Mach [TNR90] uses this approach.

---

[1] http://www.lynuxworks.com
[2] http://www.lynuxworks.com

4.1.2. Component-based Real-Time Operating Systems

Many research real-time operating systems are component-based like: OS-Kit [FBB+97], Coyote [BHSC97], DREAMS [Dit00], PURE [BGP+99], 2K [KSC+98], MMLite [HF98] or Pebble [GSB+99]. These operating systems define operating system components which can be combined to a real-time system. With this approach for a special class of applications an operating system can be created offline. Thus, the opportunity is given to eliminate unnecessary operating system components from the operating system configuration. This minimizes the overhead of the operating system itself. The operating system MMLite even allows to exchange operating system components during run-time.

4.1.3. QoS-based Real-Time Operating Systems

In soft real-time systems a miss of deadlines has no fatal consequences for the overall system. In real-time operating systems for such systems the approach of quality of service (QoS) was absorbed from the network area. Here warranties are assured to the applications at the time point of reservation of the resources. For this purpose different scheduling strategies were proposed as for example Fair-share Scheduling [JSMA98], Proportional Scheduling [SAwJ+96] or Rate-based Scheduling [JG01]. Different resource managers have been developed by the real-time research community which focus on QoS.

The **Adaptive Resource Management (ARM)** middleware [EJW+03] was especially developed to cope with unanticipated events, anomalies or overload conditions. It has been created for the use in the NASA's Earth Science vision. There, a couple of autonomous earth observing satellites monitor the conditions of the planet through a vast array of instruments. ARM is an optimization framework for embedded distributed hard real-time applications in dynamic scenarios. It uses a multi-mode model and models dynamic changes by means of arrival times, system load and quality of service. The middleware tries to maximize the system utilization by searching a feasible and optimal resource assignment. The transition between different modes is an atomic operation with a negligible switching time.

The ARM approach was one of the main inspirations for the FRM approach of this thesis. A system is seen as a dynamically allocated pool of resources. It is the job of a global scheduling policy to dispatch application tasks to all processors of the system. To handle this situation the ARM middleware autonomously determines the following: the allocation of resources (CPU, memory, communication links) to tasks, the fidelity of the data processing algorithms, the compression type to use data, when and what to download, and the interval of gathering telemetry data. The software model incorporates knowledge of *application profiles*, network hardware, *utility*, and *service level* constructs for the applications. A service level s_a is represented by a value of R. An application can have assigned a set of service levels. Additionally, each application is assigned a workload w_a. For each application a and each host h with its defined workload and service level the response time $r_{a,h}(w_a, s_a)$ and the memory consumption $m_{a,h}(w_a, s_a)$ are determined. Both $r_{a,h}$ and $m_{a,h}$ are assumed to be monotonically non-decreasing in w_a and s_a. The resource manager is responsible to find an optimal distribution of the tasks a onto host processors h. An *overall utility function* $U(s, w, r)$ can be defined, which must be monotonically non-decreasing in a combination of s, w, and r. An allocation of applications to hosts has to be found where the utility function is maximized.

This approach is applicable for example in real-time image processing – the scenario of the NASA's Earth Science vision – but not for mechatronic systems in which reconfigurations can have non negligible switching times.

The **Dynamic QoS Manager (DQM)** [BN02] implements a quality of service level module for soft real-time applications. The manager is implemented as a middleware of a general purpose operating system. The DQM optimizes the global utilization by activating the corresponding QoS level of the application. The QoS level of an application characterizes the resource requirements and the benefit of the application, when the level is executed. The resource requirements are determined through measurements at run-time. This approach is only applicable for soft real-time systems.

LEE ET AL. in [LLS+99] introduced **Q-RAM**, which uses *QoS dimensions* for a group of applications. In this approach a utility function is used in order to dynamically optimize the resource requests of dynamic *application service levels*. The model requires concrete *a priori* application profiles for each application.

LIU ET AL. in [LFA+04, FGL+04] proposed a model-driven resource management technique designed for online resource management of distributed real-time and embedded systems. They have implemented this technique in the **Quality-based Adaptive Resource Management Architecture (QARMA)**, which is implemented in the context of CORBA, and related design tools. The technique comprises a visual modeling tool used by QARMA, the specification languages it generates, as well as QARMA's underlying model and software architecture.

4.1.4. Reflective Operating Systems

To improve the reaction of the operating system, meta-information about the application requirements is needed. Operating systems which use this data in extensive manner to optimally attune themselves to the applications are called reflective ones. By identifying meta-data at run-time the system has the ability to assign system resources in a predictable way under the consideration of time response in dynamic environments. Hereby the overall system is much more flexible than statically designed systems. Additionally, reflective systems are robust according to the variance from assumptions and can better react in case of a failure, as STANKOVIC and RAMAMRITHAM describe in [SR95].

A reflective operating system kernel is **Spring** [SRN+99]. Using meta-information, which the applications have to provide, the spring operating system can give out spontaneous guaranties for the performance of the applications.

Apertos [Yok92] is a reflective operating system framework. The framework provides object / metaobject separation, a meta-hierarchy and migration. An object is a container of information and a metaobject defines the semantics of the behavior. As metaobject are objects as well, metaobjects can also have metaobjects. Thus, a set of metaobjects can be seen as a virtual machine. On this base separation and hierarchy reflectors are introduced for metaobject programming. Reflectors are a set of metaobjects which can communicate under each other to guarantee functionality for an object in case of object migration.

KON ET AL. presented in [KSC+98, KMY+05] the **2K operating system** and an Automatic Configuration Service. 2K is especially designed for rapidly changing environments. It is a reflective, component-based operating system used to manage dynamic and using adaptation. A reflective middleware layer admits on-the-fly customization through dynamic loading of new components. 2K automatically resolves dependencies between different components. 2K only supports soft real-time. Also KON ET AL. stated in [KCBC02] next-gen architectures should provide reflective architectures.

In the CORBA-based **Quality Objects (QuO) middleware** [LRA+02] applications adjust their own *service level* to improve performance. Applications react to the environment on their own accord.

4.1.5. Resource Kernel

Real-time operating systems which provide special interfaces to use system resources are called resource kernels. This interfaces allow an extended real-time access to resources. Different operations concerning resources are possible like creation/breakup/association of resource sets, creation/deletion of reservations, add/remove resources to/from resource sets or gathering of resource usage information from applications. OIKAWA and RAJUMAR in [OR99] have presented the resource kernel **Portable RK**, which provides such interfaces on different operating system platforms.

DERTOUZOS and MOK in [DM89] showed that for multi-processor systems no scheduling algorithm is optimal without a priori knowledge of the deadlines, computation times, and arrival times of the tasks. Popular algorithms like earliest deadline first and least laxity scheduling can be outperformed by other promising approaches that take resource requirements into account.

In [KMSM99a, KMSM99b, KMSM00] KALOGERAKI ET AL. categorizes their system into objects. To maximize system utilization the approach schedules this objects to the processing nodes. The resource requirements of the tasks are measured through a monitoring profiler and the objects then are scheduled to the processing nodes according their defined importance values, deadlines, computation time and measured values. As the measurements are only estimations of future allocations this approach is only suitable for soft real-time systems; for hard real-time systems this approach is not suitable. The authors developed a three-level feedback loop for the global scheduling and load balancing of distributed object invocations for CORBA. The three levels comprise (i) a least laxity scheduling on a timescale of a few milliseconds, (ii) a profiling algorithm that determines the past resource usage over a second, and (iii) cooling and heating algorithms to allocate and migrate objects over many seconds.

On the application level as well a trend to reflective behavior in resource management can be observed. Applications adapt themselves to the requests from their environment [VASP09, MS04, BPB+00, EJW+03, LRA+02]. Therefore, applications support reconfiguration of requested services. This reconfiguration helps to improve the application's QoS, which can lead into an improvement of the system's overall quality. Besides this aspect, the resource usage can be optimized. Thereby, resources that are only required for high level QoS functions can be released, when a lower level QoS is satisfying the currently requested constraints.

4.2. Real-time Scheduling

In order to guarantee real-time behavior of applications during run-time, it is important to use appropriate i.e. predictable scheduling algorithms in the real-time operating system [But04, SAA+04]. If all applications and their execution parameters (eg. the worst case execution time (WCET)) are known in the design phase, static approaches can be applied. With this approaches a schedule is calculated a priori, which assures that all application are executed before their deadlines (if possible). If the system should support dynamic applications, for which not all parameters are known at the design phase of the system, a schedule must be calculated/modified at run-time. For this purpose if new applications are added to the system or if execution parameters of existing applications are changed during run-time an acceptance test must be accomplished. This test must decide if for the changes to the task set exists a new schedule, so that for no hard real-time task a deadline is exceeded. In the case of resource reassignment, especially if the reconfiguration time is not negligible, this resource reconfiguration must be considered in the schedule, so that no hard real-time task exceeds its deadline. Also it is important to consider the overhead of the operating system as well to have an real-time operating system with temporal deterministic system calls.

Scheduling algorithms can be classified according the following parameters:

- **Soft or hard real-time:** In the field of real-time scheduling it is distinguished between soft and hard real-time scheduling. If soft real-time tasks do not meet their deadline their calculations are futile. If hard real-time tasks do not meet their deadline the consequences can be catastrophic. Common examples for the two classes are: a weather forecast for the area of soft real-time and an airbag control for hard real-time systems. For the class of soft real-time scheduling best-effort algorithms can be applied.

- **Periodic or aperiodic tasks:** Aperiodic tasks enter the system for only one execution at any time point. An example for an aperiodic task could be an interrupt request. In periodic tasks instances of the task are executed periodically. The instance of a periodic task enters the ready queue of the scheduler with a fixed frequency.

- **Preemptive/non-preemptive:** Preemptive algorithms allow a reassignment of the processor to another task by interrupting the currently executed task.

- **Static/dynamic:** In static algorithms scheduling decisions are based only on fixed application parameters. In dynamic algorithms scheduling decisions are made on dynamic parameters that can be changed during run-time.

- **Optimal/heuristic:** An algorithm is called optimal if it minimizes a given cost function defined over the task set. If no specific cost function is defined and the algorithm is said to be optimal, this means that it always finds a feasible schedule whenever one exists. A heuristic tries to search for the optimum but does not guarantee to find it.

In the following the scheduling algorithm Earliest Deadline First (EDF) and the Total Bandwidth Server, an approach to integrate aperiodic tasks into an EDF schedule, are presented. Both of them are used later in this thesis to schedule application tasks and reconfigurations of resource assignments.

4.2.1. Earliest Deadline First

The Earliest Deadline First (EDF) scheduling algorithm is a dynamic priority assignment approach. The approach schedules instances of periodic tasks when they are ready according the shortest absolute deadline of all instances that are ready. If another instance is released and has the shortest deadline it preempts the currently executed instance of another task. As the task's priority is changing according to the deadline of the task's current instances the priority assignment is dynamic. The algorithm does not consider periodicity so the jitter between executions of instances of the same task is not minimized. Instead the algorithm is optimal in the sense of feasibility and EDF minimizes the maximum lateness [Der74].

Beside the optimality the advantage of the algorithm is the complexity of the algorithm ($O(\log n)$ per task, comp. [But04, p. 51ff]) and the schedulability test. The simple schedulability test is described through the following theorem:

4. Real-time Operating Systems and Resource Management

Definition 2. *A set of periodic tasks is schedulable with EDF, iff*

$$\sum_{i=1}^{n} \frac{C_i}{T_i} \leq 1,$$

with n the number of tasks of the set, C_i the computation time of each instance of task i and T_i the period of task i.

A proof can be found in [LL73]. With this schedulability test an RTOS can check whether a task set is schedulable or not. Thus, with this test and EDF hard real-time tasks can be predictably scheduled.

EDF can also be used to schedule aperiodic tasks, it even can schedule periodic and aperiodic tasks together.

4.2.2. Total Bandwidth Server

To jointly schedule aperiodic requests and periodic tasks under hard real-time conditions with EDF a server approach can be used. In this kind of approaches, the server is a placeholder within the aperiodic requests are executed. Thus, the total utilization is partitioned between the server (U_s) and the periodic tasks (U_p).

One of the server approaches is the Total Bandwidth Server (TBS). The idea behind this approach is to assign the total bandwidth U_s of the server to an arriving aperiodic task and by this obtain an early deadline for the request. As periodic hard real-time tasks do not benefit from an early execution – for these tasks only the complete execution before their deadline is important – it is better to minimize the response time for the aperiodic requests. The following deadline assignment rule is used in the TBS approach:

Definition 3. *The deadline of the kth aperiodic request with release time r_k and computation time C_k for the TBS is given by*

$$d_k = \max(r_k, d_{k-1}) + \frac{C_k}{U_s}$$

with $d_0 = 0$.

After the deadline is assigned the aperiodic request is added to EDF scheduling queue and scheduled accordingly. SPURI and BUTTAZZO in [SB96] proved that:

Theorem 1. *Given a set of n periodic tasks with processor utilization U_p and a TBS with processor utilization U_s, the whole set is schedulable iff*

$$U_p + U_s \leq 1.$$

Thus, the TBS approach can be used to integrate the execution of aperiodic requests into the execution of hard real-time tasks, without violating any deadlines of the hard real-time tasks.

Mode Change Protocols

Systems with multiple task sets are known in literature as *multi mode systems*. A reconfiguration between two configurations is called *mode change transition* (eg. [PB98]). Through a mode change request (MCR) a crossover from one task set to another one is triggered. The crossover is accomplished by a mode change protocol. Such a protocol assesses the schedule for the crossover between the two different modes. REAL and CRESPO in [RC04] presented in their survey criteria for mode change protocols based on the requirements that are considered as goals to be achieved during the mode change transitions:

Schedulability All tasks of the old mode and of the new mode must meet their deadlines even while the mode change is performed.

Periodicity The activation pattern of tasks is not changed during a mode change. Thus, there is no jitter between the executions of task instances.

Promptness The mode change is executed immediately after the mode change is requested.

Consistency Shared resources must be used in a consistent way to avoid data corruption.

Another good survey about mode changes can be found in FĂRCAŞ in [Făr06].

4.3. Engineering Standards

In the market for embedded systems it is common that companies, that are associated via the chain of Economic Value Added (EVA) of one or multiple products, agree on a combined standard of their solution. In the area of real-time operating systems different standards exist. Some standards specify interfaces rather the functionality between operating system and applications. Other standards concentrate on the development process of dependable embedded systems, to certify a maximum of software quality. These standards can also be applied to the development process of operating systems to certify the dependability of them.

For example, the open service gateways initiative (OSGi) has created a standard for networked applications. In the automotive sector many developers use the operating system specification for car control system OSEK (German: Offene Systeme und deren Schnittstellen für die Elektronik in Kraftfahrzeugen; English: Open Systems and their Interfaces for the Electronics in Motor Vehicles). This standard has been partly published as an international standard [ISO05].

DO-178B "Software Considerations in Airborne Systems and Equipment Certification" is a norm for the development of software from the avionic area [RTC92]. The standard was developed from the RTCA (Radio Technical Commission for Aeronautics) and EUROCAE (European Organisation for

4. Real-time Operating Systems and Resource Management

Civil Aviation Equipment). The American authority FAA (Federal Aviation Administration) employs the norm for certification of software and software development processes in the area of avionic.

The IEEE standard 1003.1-2004 "Standard for Information Technology – Portable Operating System Interface (POSIX)" [IEE04] is a base definition for a standardized interface between applications and the operating system. The standard has been extended by the IEEE standard 1003.13-2003 "IEEE Standard for Information Technology- Standardized Application Environment Profile (AEP)-POSIX Real-time and Embedded Application Support" [IEE03]. This extension concentrates on the area of real-time and embedded systems. The standard uses scheduling with fixed priorities, FIFO scheduling, priority-based round-robin scheduling and scheduling with sporadic servers. Also the standard instructs the support of synchronization under the consideration of priorities as well as the budgeting of execution times of individual applications.

The Asian standard μiTron [Ker99] specifies – alike POSIX – operating system interfaces and their functionality. μiTron is used in the area of entertainment industry especially in the sector of mobile phones.

Java is a widely-used programming language in the area of desktop, internet and mobile end device. By the support of dynamic concepts (e.g. garbage collection, dynamic loading ...) in the programming language, adjustments were necessary to use Java in the area of real-time systems. The standard RTSJ [Rea05] of the Real-Time for Java Expert Group defines a set of interfaces and their behavior specification that allow real-time programming under Java. RTSJ supports soft and hard real-time. The specification enables the execution of periodic and sporadic applications und deadlines as well as the budgeting of the CPU assignment. Additionally the garbage collection can be controlled to avoid a delay in the execution of applications.

The international standard IEC 61508 [DIN02b] with the title "Functional safety of electrical/electronic/programmable electronic safety-related systems" is a basic dependability standard for different electronic systems that implement dependability features. The standard combines the complete life cycle of a product: conception, planning development, realization, commissioning, maintenance, modification the point of shutdown and uninstalling. The norm assumes that risks that affect the dependability cannot be excluded by hundred per cent. Additionally the dependability should be considered from the beginning of the product planning and not tolerable risks have to be reduced. For special areas as railway transportation additional separate standards exists, e.g. the European norm EN 50129:2003 with the title "Railway applications - Communications, signaling and processing systems - Safety related electronic systems for signaling" [BSI03].

Different automotive manufacturers and suppliers have allied to an international consortium and try to establish an open standard for the electric and IT architecture in the automotive field with AUTOSAR (AUTomotive Open System ARchitecture) [HBS$^+$06]. Core of the architecture of AU-

TOSAR is the AUTOSAR run-time environment (RTE) that abstracts from a real topology of control devices.

The programming language ADA [Bar06] is often used to program dependable embedded real-time systems. For this purpose the language is adequate because it supports special attributes to increase the dependability: e.g. type safety, run-time tests for memory overflow or simplified program verification. Since 1983 a ISO/ANSI standard exists for this programming language [ISO95].

4.4. Chapter conclusion

This chapter has summarized the state of the art in the field of this thesis. New trends in the RTOS area are going in the direction to support the requirements of self-optimizing applications, thus dynamic applications. QoS-based RTOS, Reflective OS, Resource kernels, the concept of service levels for applications and mode change protocols are fundamental paradigms used in this thesis to build a RTOS for self-optimizing applications. One major absence is the fact that most approaches reported in literature are only applicable for soft real-time systems. When they support hard real-time systems they have restrictions which are not feasible in the context of self-optimizing systems (e.g. zero time reconfigurations). As well as in Chapter 2_7 mentioned, multiple position papers attest research necessity in this area (e.g. [But06, Sch02]).

Additionally scheduling algorithms used in this thesis are introduced as well as engineering standards in the field of real-time operating systems.

Part III.

RTOS for Self-optimizing Mechatronic Systems - The Concepts

5. The Flexible Resource Manager - Concept

This chapter presents the main concept of this thesis: The Flexible Resource Manager (FRM). The main goal of the FRM is to optimize the resource utilization. Additionally, an innovative feature of this approach enables the use of spare resources under hard real-time constraints by *over-allocating the resources*.

The FRM is an operating system driven approach to achieve better resource utilization in dynamic embedded real-time systems with EDF scheduling. Under dynamic conditions, applications may have likewise dynamic resource demands. Especially in the scenario of the CRC 614, self-optimizing applications often have dynamic resource consumptions: Feedback controller with different resource usage (e.g. memory or CPU utilization) are exchanged at run-time to choose the optimal one for the situation. On the other hand, some optimization methods are not required continuously at run-time but rather depend on or triggered by environmental conditions. In classical hard real-time systems, the maximum amount of possibly required resources are held back to guarantee a timely supply by the resource manager of the operating system. This approach is not suitable for dynamic systems, because it would lead to high internal waste of resources.

First in this chapter, the general system model is introduced in Section 5.1. The basis of the concept of the Flexible Resource Manager is described afterwards in Section 5.2_{52}. At the end of the chapter, in Section 5.3_{59}, the concept is compared by means of criteria of mode change protocols and, in Section 5.4_{60}, classified into the self-optimizing concept.

5.1. General System Model

In the succeeding subsections the following system model is used, in which the Flexible Resource Manager is operating. The formal model is suitable for the hardware platform for self-optimizing applications (comp. Section 3.6_{20}), existing of a CPU inside a FPGA with a dynamic reconfiguration infrastructure. For simplification, only a single processor system in the FPGA is considered.

5.1.1. Task

A task, in literature often also referred to as process, is a computation that is executed on the CPU in a sequential fashion. $\Gamma = \{\tau_i \,|\, i = 1, 2, \ldots, n\}$ is the set of n independent tasks of the system. This means no precedence constraints are supported by the FRM, respectively synchronization between tasks must be modeled inside the tasks. The tasks can be specified as soft real-time tasks or hard real-time tasks. At the beginning it is assumed that all tasks are periodic tasks.

5.1.2. Resources

$\mathcal{R} = \{\phi_k \,|\, k = 1, 2, \ldots, m\}$ is the set of m exclusive resources that are available to the tasks in Γ. Each resource ϕ_k is only available restrictively. $U(\phi_k)$ specifies the quantitative upper bound for ϕ_k. Tasks can reserve or allocate a quota of the resources.

Most resources are only available in discrete units, resource requirements of the tasks are rounded up if they do not fit to the unit size. If a unit of a resource is used by a task, it is exclusively assigned to the task until the task releases the resource itself or is forced to do so by the FRM. Sharing a resource is only possible through the flexible resource manager. The manager enables to share the resources in a time multiplexed fashion by reassigning the resources, as described later in this thesis.

Examples for resources are: Memory, CPU utilization, reconfigurable FPGA area or network bandwidth on a communication device.

The CPU: a Special Resource

The CPU is used in a time multiplexed fashion to execute tasks in quasi parallel manner. In mechatronic systems, where the tasks can have small periods (e.g. controlling a electric motor), the CPU is reassigned frequently between the tasks down to some micro seconds. Naturally, real-time tasks have timing constraints. Execution of hard real-time tasks instances have to be finished prior to their deadlines and for soft and firm real-time tasks the execution should be finished prior to the absolute deadline of the instances. To guarantee that a task finishes its execution before the deadlines, an acceptance test based on Earliest Deadline First (EDF) (comp. Section $4.2.1_{41}$) scheduling strategy is used. Additionally, it is assumed that the deadline of a task is equal to its period. Then it is sufficient that the total CPU utilization U is equal or lower than one ($U \leq 1$) to guarantee schedulability of all tasks. Thus, the CPU utilization is handled as the resource to be allocated by tasks.

Classification of Resource Reconfiguration

For resources, like memory, the execution of application tasks has to be stopped while reassigning these resources. The reassignment is done by the resource manager, which is executed on the same CPU. But a permanent CPU access is not required for all resources while changing resource assignments. For some resources only initial work on the CPU is required. The FPGA, when considering the area of the FPGA as a resource, can be reconfigured in background in the proposed platform for self-optimizing application. From the CPU point of view the reconfiguration only has to be initiated like a DMA transfer. After the reconfiguration of the FPGA is finished and the new circuit is loaded, the task can be informed and use the circuit. Thus, most part of the reconfiguration can be done in the background while executing other tasks on the CPU and even areas on the same FPGA, which are not affected by the reconfiguration, can continue their work.

Definition 4. $\mathcal{R}_a$ *is the set of resources **actively** reconfigured by the CPU and $\mathcal{R}_p$ is the set of **passive** reconfigurable resources in background, with $\mathcal{R}_a \cap \mathcal{R}_p = \emptyset$ and $\mathcal{R}_a \cup \mathcal{R}_p = \mathcal{R}$.*

To enable that applications can continue their executions while passively requesting resource requirements, this resource request can be announced. And the application is informed when the demand resource can be used.

Reassigning the CPU utilization can (virtually) be done in the background in the same way as reconfiguring on FPGA. Changing CPU utilization of a periodic task means changing its computation time and/or its period. The FRM only uses the CPU utilization as a resource. This approach abstracts from the execution schedule. This is sufficient in the sense of schedulability, because checking the EDF schedulability criteria ($U \leq 1$) is sufficient. But the execution schedule has to be considered while reassigning the utilization between different tasks. If the CPU utilization is reassigned from a task τ_1 to another task τ_2, task τ_2 cannot, in general, start execution immediately. This is because the task τ_1 has to be considered as in a zombie state holding its old utilization until the end of its period. For example, if the time point of reassigning the utilization is after task τ_1 has been executed in its period, its part of the CPU utilization has been consumed for its current period. Until the end of the actual period of task τ_1, task τ_2 has to wait before using the CPU with the higher utilization. Otherwise the schedulability of hard real-time tasks cannot be generally guaranteed. Thus, CPU utilization is also a reconfiguration in background where other tasks can be executed on the CPU while waiting until the reassigned utilization is available again.

The release of such background reconfigurable resources is handled in the same way as actively reconfigurable resources, but the allocation takes time in the background. For an FPGA, this means the circuit is stopped immediately, the associated area is signed as free, that it can be assigned to another task, and in the background another circuit can then be loaded. For resource CPU utilization the task which gets a higher utilization assigned has to wait until utilization is available again. Thus, this task has to wait until the tasks (could be more than one) which have been used the utilization before have finished their current periods.

5.2. Flexible Resource Manager

The Flexible Resource Manager consists of two components: The *Profile Framework* and the resource manager itself. The Profile Framework builds the interface to the applications. Resources could be unused. For example, the union of all applications may not be using the whole range of resources due to their actual state. Depending on the environment, applications may have reserved resources only for some worst case scenarios but do not use them in the actual situation.

When resources are detected to be unused the resource manager of the system needs a mechanism to give resources back to be handed over to other applications of the system. Therefore, a set of applications should support several service alternatives which claim for different resource usages. This means that applications are able to change their resource usage on the resource manager's instructions. For example the resource manager can force an application to release resources up to a level specified by the application. One service alternative is called *a profile*. Due to the different resource usages per profile of an application task the quality of the application can vary. To maximize the system's quality it is the task of the resource manager to decide which application to execute in which profile. To fulfill this task under hard real-time constraints the resource manager requires additional information about the profiles of the applications and the application must stick to a special resource allocation paradigm.

5.2.1. Profile Definition

Per tasks τ_i the programmer has to define a non-empty set of profiles $P_i = \{\rho_{\tau_i,1}, ..., \rho_{\tau_i,j}\}$, with $j \geq 1$. Profiles can be compared to different *run or service levels* of a task. At each time only one profile of a task is active. $\rho_i^{\triangleright}$ terms the active profile of task τ_i. Each profile of a task implements another service level of the task. Inside of a profile the following informations are stored:

Profile Functions

Each profile comprises three executable functions:

1. *enter*-**function:** This function is called on profile activation. It initializes the profile. $W_{enter}(\rho_{\tau_i,j})$ is the WCET of this function.

5.2. Flexible Resource Manager

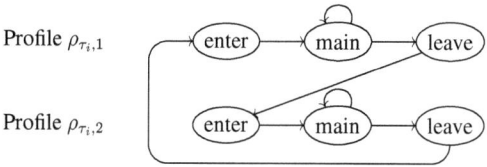

Figure 5.1.: Example function statechart for a task with two profiles

2. *main*-**function:** The *main*-function is executed periodically when the profile is active. The main functionality of the application when this profile is active is implemented in this function. $W_{main}(\rho_{\tau_i,j})$ is the WCET of this function.

3. *leave*-**function:** This function is called on profile deactivation. In this function resource allocation is forbidden, resources can only be released. The parameter of the leave function is the next profile which will be activated. $W_{leave}(\rho_{\tau_i,j})$ is the WCET of this function per period.

The state diagram in Figure 5.1 shows the transitions between the profile functions for an application with two profiles.

When switching between two profiles, the appropriate *leave*-function of the old profile will immediately be activated. If the last instance of the *main*-function of the old profile is not completely executed it will be abandoned. This means that for a consistent execution of the application the programmer has to implement appropriate abruption behavior inside the *leave*-function. Hereafter, the *enter-function* of the new profile will be executed. When the *enter*-function terminates and a delay is elapsed, the *main*-function of the new profile is inserted as new periodic task into the EDF scheduler. The delay depends on how long another task is in a zombie state after releasing CPU utilization which is assigned to this task (comp. Section 5.1.2 Classification of Resource Reconfiguration). This means a reconfiguration of profiles is done in an uninterruptible manner.

Resource Requirements

Each profile describes a different level of resource requirements of the task τ_i. A task can only allocate resources in the range that is defined by its active profile $\rho_i^\triangleright$. Thus, for every resource ϕ_k each profile $\rho_{\tau_i,j}$ needs to define a minimum quantity $\phi_{k,min}$ with $0 \leq \phi_{k,min} \leq U(\phi_k)$ as well as a maximum quantity $\phi_{k,max}$ with $\phi_{k,min} \leq \phi_{k,max} \leq U(\phi_k)$. When a task wants to allocate more resources than described in its active profile, it has to be switched by the FRM to a profile with appropriate resource requirements.

A task that has not allocated all the resources up to its maximum quantity $\phi_{k,max}$ is called a *providing task*, because it has resources which can be provided to other tasks until they are needed by the

5. The Flexible Resource Manager - Concept

providing task.

Additionally, for each resource that is passively reconfigurable, each profile defines $\phi_i \in \mathcal{R}_p$ a *maximum assignment delay* $t_{\phi_i,\text{max\_delay}}$. The delay describes the *maximum* delay between the request and the assignment of the resource. The FRM ensures that the resource is assigned after the request before this delay. As mentioned before, the FPGA and the CPU utilization are resources of this kind.

The task is responsible to release, in the leave function, as much resources so that the new upper boundaries of the next profile are not violated. For example, if the actual quantity for the resource memory of the old profile was 10 KB and the upper boundary of the next profile is 5 KB, the leave function is responsible to release 5 KB. Exception handling can be implemented on the operating system level, if the resources are not released.

To enable the Flexible Resource Manager to predict future resource requests (comp. Section 7.1$_{82}$), the task can – but has not to – specify additional information: If the task has knowledge about its resource requirements for the resource ϕ_k within a profile $\rho_{\tau_i,j}$ in form of discrete steps $\phi_{k,1} = \phi_{k,\min}, ..., \phi_{k,l} = \phi_{k,\max} \in [\phi_{k,\min}, \phi_{k,\max}]$, with $l \in \mathbb{N}$, these steps can be specified within the profile. If additionally the discrete probability distribution is known, it can be declared as a probability mass function $F\rho_{\tau_i,j}, \phi_k(x)$. If it is known that an application variable has an effect on the resource requirements, this variables can be specified to be used as application specific information. The dependency of these variables to the resource usage is specified as a Dynamic Bayesian Network (DBN) (comp. Section 7.1$_{82}$).

The FRM itself does not support that the units of the resources are assigned contiguously to the application, it only manages the quantity. Contiguous assignment of the resource units can be achieved through special mechanisms on other abstraction levels. E.g. memory: When having a memory management unit (MMU), which supports address translation, the FRM can assign memory in the resolution of page size. Non contiguous physical memory pages can then be contiguously mapped into the virtual address space of the task.

CPU utilization As mentioned above, the CPU is a special resource. The tasks can allocate indirectly CPU utilization through the resource manager. The utilization U is calculated out of the two parameters C (the computation time each periodic instance of the task) and T (the period of a task), with $U = C/T$. Therefore per profile $\rho_{\tau_i,j}$ a task has to specify a computation time $C_{\rho_{\tau_i,j}}$, which is the WCET $W_{main}(\rho_{\tau_i,j})$ and a period $T_{\rho_{\tau_i,j}}$, which is the period of the *main*-function of this profile.

To extract more time for profile reconfiguration, tasks can specify an omit factor $o(\rho_{\tau_i,j})$ per profile, with $0 \leq o(\rho_{\tau_i,j}) \in \mathbb{N}$. This factor specifies how often a periodic instance of a task can be left out. For example, soft real-time tasks can specify this factor with a high value. But even some hard real-time tasks can be left out for a short while, for example hard real-time control tasks (comp. Section 3.6$_{20}$).

5.2. Flexible Resource Manager

Some applications need to be informed after the omission about the number of omissions. Thus, this information is provided to the main function of the profile.

Profile Transitions

The FRM is responsible for activating a profile, but the application can specify per profile to which other profiles a switch is allowed. $P_{trans}(\rho_{\tau_i,j}) \subset P_i$ is the subset of profiles which can be activated from $\rho_{\tau_i,j}$.

Minimum Dwell Time

Per profile, a minimum dwell time t_d can be specified. If a profile is activated by the FRM, a transition to another profile is forbidden until the minimum dwell time is elapsed.

Profile Quality

The programmer (offline), the task itself or a quality manager application (online) can order the profiles according to their quality. The quality of a profile ρ is defined through the quality value $q_\rho \in [0,1]$. The FRM uses this value to decide which profile to activate as described in detail later.

5.2.2. Profile Configuration

A combination of profiles $c = (\rho_1, \rho_2, ..., \rho_n)$ with $\rho_1 \in P_1, \rho_2 \in P_2, ..., \rho_n \in P_n$ is called the configuration of the system. This means every configuration maps each task to one of its profiles. The configuration of all actual profiles $c^\triangleright = (\rho_1^\triangleright, \rho_2^\triangleright, ..., \rho_n^\triangleright)$ is called active configuration.

Configuration Classification

Configurations can be classified into different sets according to their overall feasibility and partial feasibility (comp. Figure 5.2_{56}):

Feasible & infeasible configuration Not every configuration is feasible. If the sum of all minimal resource requirements of the profiles of a configuration exceed the amount of resource available in the system the configuration cannot be activated. Activation is not possible – even if all tasks allocate only the minimal specified resources – as not all resource requests could be assigned.

5. The Flexible Resource Manager - Concept

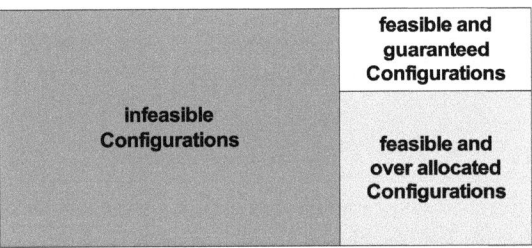

Figure 5.2.: Set diagram of configurations

Definition 5. *A configuration $c \in C$ is feasible when for all $\phi_k \in \mathcal{R}$ it holds that*

$$\sum_{i=1}^{|\Gamma|} \phi_{k,\min}(\rho_{\tau_i}) \leq U(\phi_k).$$

If a configuration c is not feasible it is called infeasible.

Guaranteed allocation Per configuration, a resource is defined to be in a guaranteed allocation state, when the normalized sum of all upper bounds of the resource requirements of the profiles of the configuration is lower than 100%. The configuration is defined to be in a guaranteed allocation state, when all resources are in a guaranteed allocation state. In such a configuration all resource requirements – up to the upper bound of the profiles – can be granted at once.

Definition 6. *A configuration $c \in C$ is in a guaranteed state when c is feasible and for all $\phi_k \in \mathcal{R}$ it holds that*

$$\sum_{i=1}^{|\Gamma|} \phi_{k,\max}(\rho_{\tau_i}) \leq U(\phi_k).$$

Over-allocation In a real-time environment, an application needs guaranteed resources. Thus, resources are normally reserved for worst-case resource allocations. In the average case this leads to unused resources.

Per configuration a resource is to be defined in an over-allocation state, when not all upper bounds of the resource requirements of the configuration can be granted at the same time. This means that the sum of all upper bounds of the resource requirements for the resource exceeds the available amount of the resource in the system. In other words, a configuration is to be defined in an over-allocation state, when one or more resources are in an over-allocation state.

5.2. Flexible Resource Manager

When a conflict appears (more resources are required than available) this conflict must be solved, because in a real-time environment the applications need planning reliability. Denying of a resource requirement is normally not acceptable and can lead into catastrophic results. To deal with this fact the FRM allows transitions from a guaranteed allocation configuration to an over-allocation configuration only under special circumstances. Transitions can only be granted if a guaranteed allocation configuration can be reached in time, when a conflict appears. Thus, a predictable behavior/plan has to exist to solve a possible conflict before an over-allocation state is activated.

Definition 7. *A configuration $c \in C$ is in an over-allocated state when c is feasible, but not in a guaranteed state.*

5.2.3. Quality of the System

The FRM is responsible for switching between the profiles of the tasks under the switching conditions. To provide the FRM with information, which profile is best for an application and which application to favor, the FRM considers the quality of the profile and the importance ($\iota_i \in [0,1]$) of each task τ_i.

This parameter represents the importance of this task within the whole system and the FRM can consider it for optimizing the system. The value is set from the programmer, but can be changed dynamically at runtime.

A quality function $Q(c)$ defines the quality of a configuration. The FRM uses this function to decide which configuration has to be activated, by maximizing the quality function. The programmer of the system has to define the quality function. For example, a simple quality function can be:

$$Q(c) = \sum_{\tau \in \Gamma} \iota_\tau \cdot q_{\rho_\tau}, \text{ with } \rho_\tau \in c$$

5.2.4. Profile Reachability Graph

A *profile reachability configuration graph* can be defined from the profile information of the tasks. This is a directed graph (C, T). Each configuration $c \in C$ represents a node. From one node to another node a directed edge $t \in T$ exists, if and only if the system can switch from the first to the second configuration. A weight, which indicates how long it takes to switch from the source to the destination configuration, is assigned to the edges. This weight is the sum of all WCETs of the enter and leave methods of the corresponding profiles which change between this two configurations. Each node is classified to be in a guaranteed allocation state or an over-allocation state. This classification can also be done per resource.

5. The Flexible Resource Manager - Concept

5.2.5. Allowing Over-Allocation

As mentioned above in an over-allocation state a conflict can arise, which has to be solved under hard real-time conditions. The basic idea is to allow the system to be in an over-allocation state configuration, when the FRM can ensure that a guaranteed allocation state configuration can be reached in time. Thus, resource conflicts are solved by forcing the system to another profile configuration in which the conflict is solved. By forcing a profile transition of some applications from a profile with a higher resource consumption to a profile with a lower resource consumption the applications have to free the resources in the leave-methods of the leaved profiles. The application, which requested resources and caused the conflict, can be forced as well to a profile with lower resource requirements. Of course, this could only happen if it has such a profile and it is reachable from the current one. This would mean an indirect decline of the request.

The reachability of a guaranteed allocation *in time* means that the immediate profile reconfiguration does not cause a violation of deadlines of any real-time application of the system and all requested passive reconfigurable resources can be provided within the maximum assignment delays of the applications, specified in the profiles. Therefore, special schedulability criteria must be fulfilled to allow an over-allocation. This criteria are described in Section 6.1_{63} in detail.

For every possible conflict the FRM needs a plan to solve it. A basic approach is to have only one plan, which brings the system in a guaranteed allocation state. In such a guaranteed allocation no conflict can arise, because all resource requirements can be granted at once (comp. Definition 6_{56}). A more advanced strategy is to have more plans, to solve different conflicts better. For example, it could be enough to switch to another over-allocated configuration, if only a small portion of a resource has to be freed to solve the conflict. But in this case a second conflict could arise shortly after the first conflict. In such a case even a sequence of reconfiguration has to be checked for schedulability.

5.2.6. Dynamic of Profile Values

Profile parameters are not fixed, a change can be allowed under special circumstances. As the parameters are used by the FRM to make guarantees for hard real-time tasks, the parameters can only be changed after an acceptance test of the FRM. The test guarantees that no deadlines are violated and guaranteed resource requests can be fulfilled within the specified maximum assignment delay. So, changes of profile parameters can be declined by the resource manager. The FRM forbids the change of parameters if it would lead to an impossible system configuration or if the system is in an over-allocation state and the change would violate the current plan to solve conflicts and no new plan could be found. Profiles can be deleted and added at run-time. Deletion of a profile requires also an acceptance test, which has to check whether a feasible and guaranteed allocation configuration exists.

Adding new profiles does not require a test, as the profile is not activated directly. As any acceptance test takes time, a change cannot be granted immediately.

For changing the profile quality no acceptance test is required. The quality value is only used to guide the optimization direction and is not used to guarantee resource allocations.

5.3. Comparison to Mode Change Protocols

The Flexible Resource Manager can be seen as a mode change protocol (comp. Section $4.2.2_{43}$). The FRM considers that tasks can have different worst-case execution times in different operating modes (profiles). REAL and CRESPO in [RC04] mention that this leads into a more complicated schedulability analysis. To compensate this, the FRM requires deadlines equal to periods, i.e. $D_i = T_i$. Deadlines equal to periods simplify the EDF schedulability analysis. Next, the FRM is classified acording to the mode change categories:

Schedulability: A mode change protocol supports schedulability, if all deadlines are met even during mode change transitions. The FRM supports schedulability.

Periodicity: The FRM does not support periodicity as a goal, where the activation pattern is constant for all instances of a task. As the FRM uses EDF as scheduling strategy even in normal execution, periodicity is not guaranteed. Sampler, regulator or actuator tasks of mechatronic control systems require periodicity in their I/O. To deal with this contradictory requirements special hardware (eg. a FPGA) is used in order to buffer the I/O. The hardware performs the I/O at periodic time instances, e.g. reading sensor data or sending new output values to actuators. With this technique the calculation can be executed at an arbitrary point in time on the CPU between the I/O, namely between two activations of two instances of the task.

Promptness: The FRM supports an immediate mode change (reconfiguration due to exhaustion as described later in Chapter 6_{63}). This very prompt response is obtained by reserving time for the mode change (reconfiguration). This is the main difference in contrast to most mode change protocols presented in the survey of REAL and CRESPO.

Consistency: In the FRM concept resources are only shared in the over-allocated configurations. In case of a conflict the resources are immediately returned to the original task by forcing the system to a guaranteed allocation configuration. Some tasks are immediately forced to change their profiles. The profile transitions are responsible to free the resources in a consistent way.

Additionally it should be mentioned that the FRM maybe aborts some tasks during reconfiguration and calls their leave-functions. Therefore, this abortion is controlled by the application due to application-specific leave-functions. These functions could implement a completion of the aborted task (but without additional resource allocation).

5.4. The FRM - A Self Optimizing System

The FRM can be seen as a self-optimizing system. Figure 5.3_{61} depicts how the different operations of the FRM can be mapped into the three activities of a self-optimizing process (comp. Definition 1_{16} in Chapter 3_{15}).

Analysis of the current situation: In this stage information from the applications is collected. The situation is analyzed by obtaining information from the applications profiles and the current resource consumption of each application. Based upon this information possible configurations are calculated and possible cases of reactions (for example solving over-allocated conflicts) are identified. The calculation of probabilities for possible incidents (eg. allocation of resources, creation of new applications, ...) can be assigned to this self-optimizing phase.

Determination of the system objectives: The optimization process inside the FRM can be seen as determination of new objectives, because in this phase a new strategy for profile configuration is calculated. The inherent objective of the FRM is to maximize the overall system quality by utilizing the resources with a good profile combination.

Adaptation of the system behavior: The adaptation of the system behavior is done by activating/deactiviating profiles. By changing profiles the behavior of the system can also be changed, for e.g. if a different controller is activated.

5.5. Chapter Conclusion

This chapter builds the basis for the FRM, by defining the terminology used in this thesis and presenting the basic principle of resource allocation. Based on the general system model, the profile interface is defined. The profile interface enables the tasks to specify implementation alternatives with different resource requirements. On the one hand, a profile defines the ranges of resource a task is executed within, when the profile is active. On the other hand, defining more than one profile enables the FRM to assign temporarily freed resources to a task, by forcing the task to a profile which can consume the free resources. The comparison to mode change protocols sorts the FRM concept into the field of dynamic real-time systems. As the FRM supports mode changes, the requirements of self-optimizing

5.5. Chapter Conclusion

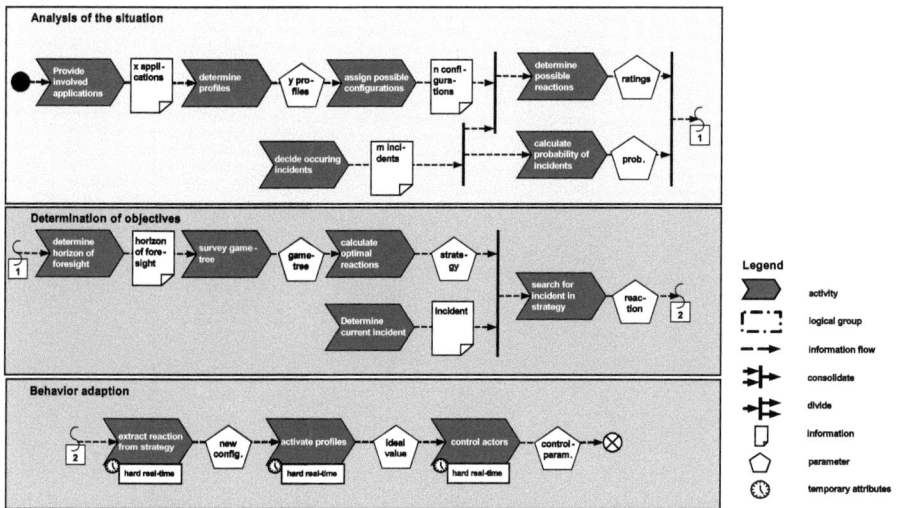

Figure 5.3.: The FRM as a self-optimizing system: Behavior – activity

applications for support for multi mode is achieved (comp. Section $3.9.1_{33}$). In the last section is shown that the FRM can be seen as a self-optimizing system.

5. The Flexible Resource Manager - Concept

6. The Flexible Resource Manager - Analysis

The last chapter has introduced the main concept behind the FRM. This chapter formally proves that the concept is working. To fulfill resource management under hard real-time constrains, the system has to fulfill two characteristics: schedulability and deadlock-freeness. In this chapter is proven that this two characteristics are fulfilled by the FRM approach.

6.1. Scheduling of Profile Reconfiguration

The schedulability analysis in presence of the FRM is a complex task. An ordinary real-time system is characterized by a unique set of tasks Γ for which schedulability must be verified. In contrast, the FRM introduces a set of configurations C in which the different profiles of a task relate to different WCETs. As a consequence, for each configuration $c_i \in C$ there exists a unique task set $\Gamma(c_i)$ with unique WCET for which schedulability must be verified. Furthermore, a schedule that contains a reconfiguration from one configuration to another is unique for every pair of configurations. Different transitions involve different profiles, and with every profile having specific WCET for its *enter/main/leave*-functions, the resulting schedule has unique characteristics, thus, yielding a unique $\Gamma(c_a, c_b)$.

In general, schedulability analysis has to be performed online. It is not advisable to verify the schedulability for the entire system a priori due to the complexity of the problem. The number of profiles per task $|P_i|$ is upper-bounded by $n_p = \max(|P_1|, \ldots, |P_i|)$. With $|\Gamma|$ tasks running in the dynamic real-time system, the maximum number of possible configurations is $n_p^{|\Gamma|}$. In the worst case, a reconfiguration between each configuration is allowed, thus having $n_p^{|\Gamma|}(n_p^{|\Gamma|} - 1)$ possible reconfigurations. Schedulability analysis of the entire system would require to verify the feasibility of characteristic schedules of the $\mathcal{O}(n_p^{|\Gamma|})$ reconfigurations.

However, there are cases in which an a priori schedulability analysis is required, when using dynamic resource management via the FRM:

Analyzing guaranteed configuration The schedulability analysis of a guaranteed configuration does not need to consider reconfiguration because a guaranteed configuration, per se, does not require reconfiguration due to a resource conflict. If the guaranteed configuration yields a feasible schedule, the system can be safely run in this configuration. The schedulability of the initial configuration must be verified offline before the system is started. All other guaranteed configurations should be verified online before they are executed. This point is refined later in this chapter.

Analyzing reconfiguration due to optimization The FRM provides an optimization algorithm that searches for a configuration with a better quality. This algorithm is executed as a task without any timing constraints. Therefore, the idle task of the RTOS lends itself to execute the optimization algorithm. Reconfiguration is performed as soon as the optimization algorithm has found a better configuration, it has assured that it can be activated and an uninterruptible reconfiguration to the new configuration can be scheduled. As the reconfiguration is only due to optimization it has not to be executed immediately. This reconfiguration process will be referred to as *reconfiguration due to optimization*. It can be initiated when the system is either in a guaranteed configuration or in an over-allocated configuration. If the schedule of a guaranteed configuration is too tight to allow for an uninterruptible reconfiguration process, then the system will never be optimized, although that configuration can be executed. To avoid this, if not enough idle time for the reconfiguration exists a two step approach is used: First, instances of soft real-time tasks are left out and second, if this is not enough, hard real-time tasks are left out if an omit factor greater than zero is specified. This is applicable because the FRM tries to keep the number of reconfigurations at an acceptable rate. In any case, only instances of tasks are left out if it is allowed by the specified omit factor. This is decided by the FRM which can plan the schedule some time instances ahead to see, whether a gap of idle time exists with or without leaving task instances out. If no gap in a specified time boundary exists, even if some task instance would be left out, it is searched for another configuration.

Analyzing reconfiguration due to exhaustion The optimization algorithm may suggest a guaranteed or an over-allocated configuration for reconfiguration. The properties of schedulability analysis for a guaranteed configuration have been discussed briefly. For an over-allocated configuration, another form of reconfiguration must be considered to occur during the execution of every instance of a providing task. This kind of reconfiguration process is referred to as *reconfiguration due to exhaustion*. If a providing task needs to allocate a resource that is currently held by tasks executing in their optimized profiles, the conflict must be solved. For example, a basic strategy is that reconfiguration must return to a guaranteed configuration so that the request of the providing task can be satisfied. Before an over-allocated configuration can be activated, the schedulability analysis must check in case of the basic strategy whether the new configuration is including a reconfiguration back to a guaranteed configuration and produces a feasible schedule. Therefore, the schedulability analysis must assure that reconfiguration due to exhaustion does not violate any timing constraints. This schedulability analysis must be performed online before activating an over-allocated configuration that has been suggested by the optimization algorithm of the FRM. If a more advanced strategy is used, which reconfigures to another over-allocated configuration to solve the conflict, there must exist a plan, to which configuration to reconfigure in case of a second conflict, and so on. In this case for all possible reconfigurations and configurations of the plan schedulability must be checked in advance.

In the following, a formal schedulability analysis is presented for the three classes listed above. For the following analysis it must be emphasized that reconfiguration is to be treated as an *atomic* and non interrupted process. This is required because any resource allocation during an interrupted reconfiguration process may operate on invalid data, thus endangers the predictability of the entire system.

6.1.1. Analyzing Guaranteed Configurations

The processor utilization of any configuration c is determined by the WCET and the period of the periodically executed *main*-functions of all profiles $\rho \in c$ (comp. Section 5.2.1$_{53}$). Hence, the total processor utilization can be defined as:

Definition 8. *The processor utilization $U(c)$ of a configuration $c = (\rho_{\tau_1}, \rho_{\tau_2}, \ldots, \rho_{\tau_n}) \in C$ is given by*

$$U(c) = \sum_{i=1}^{n} \frac{W_{\text{main}}(\rho_{\tau_i})}{T_i}.$$

It has to be mentioned that $U(c)$ only considers the utilization induced by the *main*-functions of the periodic tasks. $U(c)$ is sufficient to determine the feasibility of a schedule produced by a guaranteed configuration c. Its feasibility can be verified by the following theorem:

Theorem 2. *A guaranteed configuration $c \in C_g$ can be feasibly scheduled under EDF if it holds that*

$$U(c) \leq 1.$$

Proof. For any configuration $c \in C$, the WCET of the task τ_i is specified in its profile $\rho_{\tau_i} \in c$ by the WCET of the *main*-function. Since it is assumed that the configuration c is guaranteed, no immediate reconfiguration due to a resource conflict is required that would increase the response time of any task. Therefore, the theorem follows from the EDF schedulability bound of one (comp. Section 4.2.1$_{41}$).
∎

6. The Flexible Resource Manager - Analysis

Theorem 2 must be used to determine the schedulability of the initial configuration c_s before the system is run. The remaining guaranteed configurations $C_g - \{c_s\}$ need not to be analyzed in advance, but must be analyzed online whenever the optimization algorithm decides to activate one of it.

6.1.2. Analyzing Reconfiguration Due to Optimization

For any analysis involving reconfiguration, the WCET of a reconfiguration process is needed. As mentioned in the beginning of Section 6.1_{63}, this WCET is unique for every transition $c_a \to c_b$ and can be defined as follows:

Definition 9. *The worst case execution time $W_\mathrm{reconf}(c_a, c_b)$ for a reconfiguration $c_a \to c_b$ is given by*

$$W_\mathrm{reconf}(c_a, c_b) = \sum_{\rho \in c_a} W_\mathrm{leave}(\rho) + \sum_{\rho \in c_b} W_\mathrm{enter}(\rho).$$

After the optimization algorithm has found a better configuration, the reconfiguration process must be integrated into the current schedule. On the one hand, reconfiguration must not cause any deadlines to be missed in the new configuration. On the other hand, the reconfiguration process must not be interrupted. Reconfiguration can be regarded as an aperiodic request that is to be executed after any periodic instance, but only if it can be guaranteed that no interruption will occur. The FRM can select the time point of the reconfiguration as described earlier in this chapter.

Whenever aperiodic requests need to be integrated into a periodic schedule, priority servers can be used. For reconfiguration due to optimization, the total remaining processing power to the reconfiguration process needs to be assigned. Therefore, the concept of the Total Bandwidth Server (TBS) (comp. Section $4.2.2_{42}$) for the assignment is used. For the following description, assume that reconfiguration has to perform the transition $c_a \to c_b$ where c_a is the current configuration and c_b has been selected by the optimization algorithm. The bandwidth that can be used for the TBS is equal to the difference between the current processor utilization $U(c_a)$ to full utilization, thus

$$U_s = 1 - U(c_a).$$

The deadline for the reconfiguration process is based on the TBS deadline assignment rule (com. Definition 3_{42}). In this specific case, only a single reconfiguration is considered, thus only one aperiodic request. If it is demand that no successive reconfiguration occurs due to optimization before the deadline of the pending reconfiguration has been reached, the $\max(\cdot)$-function in the Definition 3_{42} is not necessary anymore. If a reconfiguration $c_a \to c_b$ due to optimization begins at time t_r and is completed within $W_\mathrm{reconf}(c_a, c_b)$ time, then the deadline d_r of the reconfiguration process is given by

$$d_r = t_r + \frac{W_\mathrm{reconf}(c_a, c_b)}{1 - U(c_a)}.$$

6.1. Scheduling of Profile Reconfiguration

The knowledge of the deadline d_r is important because it must be assured that reconfiguration is not interrupted. This can only be guaranteed if at time t there is no other task τ_i pending with a deadline $d_i < d_r$. To assure that $d_i \geq d_r$ the FRM uses the following two important points:

1. *No timing constraints are violated* – The reconfiguration is treated as an aperiodic request served by a TBS. Thus, according to Theorem 3 of SPURI and BUTTAZZO in [SB96] the set of periodic tasks including the reconfiguration process is schedulable.

2. *Reconfiguration is atomic* – The FRM is able to detect an interruption of the reconfiguration process in advance by comparing deadlines, and, in such a case, would not start a reconfiguration. Thus, if a reconfiguration occurs due to optimization, it is atomic.

With this approach, reconfiguration due to optimization is treated as an aperiodic job that is scheduled by the EDF scheduler of the RTOS just like an ordinary task. Possible preemptions can be detected in advance by comparing the assigned deadlines to the pending deadlines of the periodic tasks. As mentioned earlier, tasks can be left out in a controlled manner when they have specified an omit factor to increase the time, which can be used, due to optimization, for an atomic reconfiguration.

6.1.3. Analyzing Reconfiguration Due to Exhaustion

In an over-allocated configuration, a providing task may have to use resources that are held by other tasks. However, a plan – reconfiguring to another profile configuration – exists to solve the conflict. If that configuration is activated, the resource in question will be (partially) released, and the providing task can safely allocate the resources it needs. In contrast to reconfiguration due to optimization, where reconfiguration is only scheduled if it cannot be interrupted, here reconfiguration must be scheduled upon unfulfillable resource requests of providing tasks. Thus, the reconfiguration has to be executed immediately. Then, reconfiguration must not be interrupted. The difference is that in the former case, the time for reconfiguration can be chosen while in the latter one reconfiguration must take place immediately. The strategy described for reconfiguration due to optimization cannot be used here since it is impossible to wait for a moment that allows an atomic reconfiguration.

Before the new strategy is derived, it is illustrated why interruptions can occur. Figure 6.1$_{68}$ illustrates the problem of interruption. Reconfiguration is initiated by task τ_r due to an unfulfillable resource request at time t_r. The deadline of the instance $\tau_{r,i}$ that caused reconfiguration is $d_{r,i}$. Since reconfiguration is executed on behalf of τ_r, the process of reconfiguration is executed under the same deadline $d_{r,i}$. Interruptions during reconfiguration will occur if periodic instances of tasks other than τ_r are released after t_r with a deadline less than $d_{r,i}$ and before reconfiguration has completed. In this example, τ_a is released at $t_r < d_{a,j-1} < t_r + W_{\text{reconf}}$ with a deadline $d_{a,j} < d_{r,i}$, thus the EDF

6. The Flexible Resource Manager - Analysis

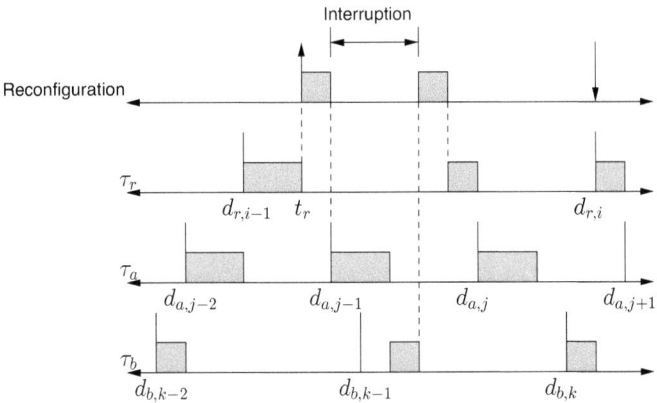

Figure 6.1.: Under EDF scheduling, reconfiguration on behalf of a providing task τ_r may be interrupted by tasks of which periodic instances are released during reconfiguration with a deadline less than that of τ_r.

scheduler will interrupt τ_r and its reconfiguration process in favor of τ_a. If instances of other tasks are yet released, they may incur further interruptions. In the example, another task τ_b is also released during reconfiguration. With $d_{a,j} < d_{b,k} < d_{r,i}$ it will be executed immediately after the instance of τ_a has completed, thus further prolonging the interruption during reconfiguration.

A simple solution to this problem is illustrated in Figure 6.2₆₉. By assigning the deadline $d^*_{r,i} = t_r + W_{\text{reconf}}$ to the reconfiguration process, it becomes the highest priority job in the example. It then holds that $d^*_{r,i} < d_{a,j} < d_{b,k} < d_{r,i}$, so reconfiguration is executed first without any interruption, then the instances of τ_a and τ_b are executed, and finally the remainder of τ_r completes. However, three open questions need to be answered for this solution to be acceptable in general.

1. Is it true that with this deadline assignment reconfiguration indeed becomes atomic, or is it just coincidence that it works for this example and may not hold in general?

2. The new deadline $d^*_{r,i}$ postpones the execution of τ_a and τ_b. Such deferral could cause future deadlines to be missed. What restrictions need to be installed so that it can be guaranteed that for arbitrary configurations no timing constraints are violated?

3. Is the deadline for reconfiguration really the shortest and the reconfiguration executed immediately or could the providing task which causes the reconfiguration through a resource allocation be executed so late that it would have a shorter deadline? Thus, is it always true that: $d^*_{r,i} < d_{r,i}$?

6.1. Scheduling of Profile Reconfiguration

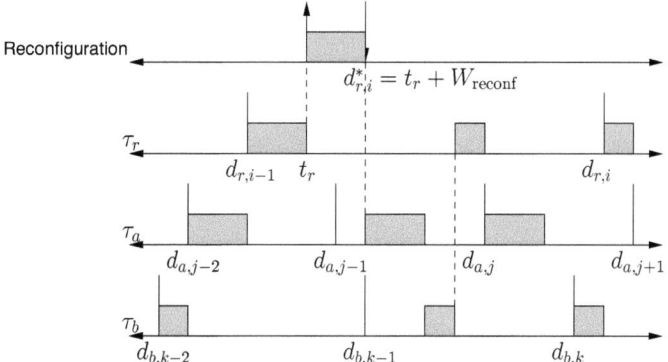

Figure 6.2.: Reconfiguration can be made atomic by assigning it a deadline that makes it the highest priority job.

The atomicity of reconfiguration due to exhaustion can be guaranteed by Lemma 1 under the assumption that it is immediately executed.

Lemma 1. *Reconfiguration due to exhaustion at time t_r with the deadline assignment $t_r + W_{\text{reconf}}$ is atomic if $T_i \geq W_{\text{reconf}}$ holds for all tasks $\tau_i \in \Gamma$.*

Proof. In the following, τ_r refers to the providing task that initiates reconfiguration, and t_r is the absolute moment in time at which reconfiguration begins. Let $\tau_{r,i}$ denote the ith instance that initiates reconfiguration and let $d_{r,i}$ be its absolute deadline.

Lemma 1 is proven by contradiction. Assume that for all tasks $\tau_i \in \Gamma$ it holds that $T_i \geq W_{\text{reconf}}$ and yet reconfiguration with the deadline assignment

$$d^*_{r,i} = t_r + W_{\text{reconf}} \qquad (6.1)$$

is not atomic. All task instances that could possibly interfere with reconfiguration are released after t_r because at time t_r, τ_r needs to be executed in order to initiate reconfiguration. If τ_r is executing at time t_r, then at t_r it must be the task with the earliest deadline among all ready instances. Otherwise, it would not be executing according to the EDF policy. For a task $\tau_i \neq \tau_r$ to interfere with reconfiguration, there must exist an instance $\tau_{i,x}$ that is released after t_r with an absolute deadline $d_{i,x}$ less than $d^*_{r,i}$ (Equation 6.1). Otherwise, the EDF scheduler would not preempt the reconfiguration process. Thus, the release time $r_{i,x}$ of the interfering instance $\tau_{i,x}$ is bounded by

$$t_r < r_{i,x} < t_r + W_{\text{reconf}}.$$

6. The Flexible Resource Manager - Analysis

In other words, the interfering instance must be released at

$$r_{i,x} = t_r + \Delta \text{ with } 0 < \Delta < W_{\text{reconf}}. \tag{6.2}$$

Under the assumption $D_i = T_i$, it holds for the absolute deadline that

$$d_{i,x} = r_{i,x} + T_i \stackrel{6.2}{=} t_r + \Delta + T_i. \tag{6.3}$$

With $d_{i,x} < d^*_{r,i}$, Equation 6.1₆₉ and Equation 6.3 can be substituted, yielding

$$t_r + \Delta + T_i < t_r + W_{\text{reconf}}$$

and, thus,

$$T_i < W_{\text{reconf}} - \Delta.$$

T_i is maximized for $\Delta = 0$. In consequence, reconfiguration with the deadline assignment given by Equation 6.1₆₉ can only be interrupted if there exists at least one task with a period less than W_{reconf}. However, it was assumed that all tasks have periods greater than or equal to W_{reconf}, which is a contradiction. ∎

Lemma 1₆₉ guarantees atomicity of reconfiguration, but it does not answer the question whether schedulability can be guaranteed. Before another restriction that guarantees the schedulability can be derived, the result of Lemma 1₆₉ needs to be extended to the more general case of $W_{\text{reconf}} + \lambda$. The λ-increment will be required later when the schedulability is proven by using the TBS. Without the extension the reconfiguration would only be feasibly scheduled when the complete CPU utilization would be reserved for reconfiguration, thus $U_s = 1$. In other words, for the utilization for the hard real-time tasks would be $U_p = 0$. Thus, without a $\lambda 0$ no application could use the CPU if a reconfiguration due to exhaustion could happen, which is proven inside the proof of Lemma 2₇₁.

Corollary 1. *Reconfiguration due to exhaustion at time t_r with the deadline assignment $t_r + W_{\text{reconf}} + \lambda$ is atomic if $T_i \geq W_{\text{reconf}} + \lambda$ with $\lambda > 0$ holds for all tasks $\tau_i \in \Gamma$.*

Proof. Corollary 1 can be proven using the same approach as for Lemma 1₆₉. The duration of reconfiguration is extended by the increment λ, thus by using $W_{\text{reconf}} = W'_{\text{reconf}} + \lambda$ with W'_{reconf} being the actual time required for reconfiguration, the corollary follows. ∎

Figure 6.3₇₁ illustrates the meaning of the λ-increment. The interval $[t_r, t_r + W'_{\text{reconf}} + \lambda]$ is treated as the entire reconfiguration process, although the actual reconfiguration process is smaller. Corollary 1 is required for the proof of the following lemma, which guarantees the schedulability of reconfiguration due to exhaustion.

6.1. Scheduling of Profile Reconfiguration

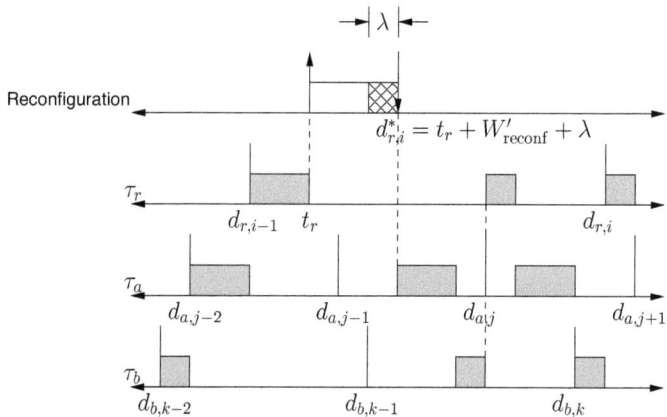

Figure 6.3.: The process of reconfiguration is enlarged artificially by the λ-increment.

Lemma 2. *An over-allocated configuration $c_a \in C_o$ with a possible reconfiguration to the guaranteed configuration $c_b \in C_g$ can be feasibly scheduled under EDF if it holds that*

$$U_p \leq 1 - \frac{W_{\text{reconf}}(c_a, c_b)}{W_{\text{reconf}}(c_a, c_b) + \lambda}$$

with $U_p = \max\{U(c_a), U(c_b)\}$ and $\lambda \geq 0$.

Proof. The idea of the proof is again to treat the reconfiguration process as an aperiodic job and reuse the scheduling criteria of the TBS approach. The criteria of the TBS is to assign the deadlines of the aperiodic request according to Definition 3₄₂, which for a single reconfiguration request – as in this case – becomes

$$d_k = r_k + \frac{C_k}{U_s}. \tag{6.4}$$

Recalling the scenario depicted in Figure 6.3, reconfiguration begins at time $r_k = t_r$ with the assigned deadline $d_k = t_r + W_{\text{reconf}}(c_a, c_b) + \lambda$. The execution time of reconfiguration is $C_k = W_{\text{reconf}}(c_a, c_b)$. To guarantee schedulability, by reusing the TBS schedulability criteria, the assigned deadline and the deadline rule of the TBS approach are set equal. Thus, by substituting the expressions for r_k, d_k, and C_k in Equation 6.4 following equation is evolved:

$$t_r + W_{\text{reconf}}(c_a, c_b) + \lambda = t_r + \frac{W_{\text{reconf}}(c_a, c_b)}{U_s}. \tag{6.5}$$

Solving this equation for the bandwidth U_s of the TBS yields

$$U_s = \frac{W_{\text{reconf}}(c_a, c_b)}{W_{\text{reconf}}(c_a, c_b) + \lambda}. \tag{6.6}$$

6. The Flexible Resource Manager - Analysis

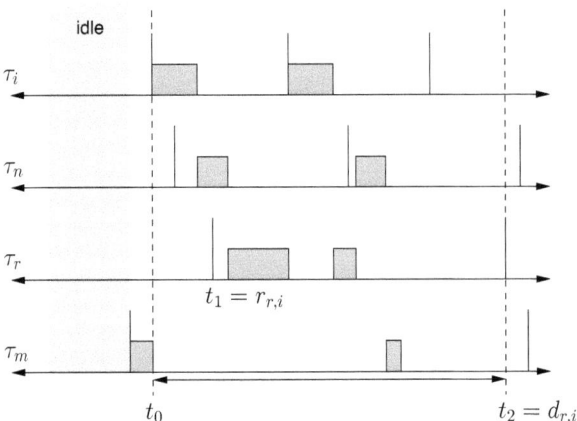

Figure 6.4.: Example schedule to illustrate the proof of Lemma 3

Since schedulability needs to be guaranteed, according to Theorem 3 of SPURI and BUTTAZZO in [SB96], the set of periodic tasks and the aperiodic request, i.e., the reconfiguration process, is schedulable if and only if $U_p + U_s \leq 1$. Substituting Equation 6.6 yields the proposition:

$$U_p \leq 1 - \frac{W_{\text{reconf}}(c_a, c_b)}{W_{\text{reconf}}(c_a, c_b) + \lambda} \qquad (6.7)$$

∎

It is to be mentioned that for any two configurations c_a and c_b $W_{\text{reconf}}(c_a, c_b)$ and U_p are known. Thus, in Inequation 6.7 λ is the only unknown variable and a bound can be calculated.

The next general lemma is used later to show why the reconfiguration can be executed immediately, without violating the deadline of the task which caused the reconfiguration. The question is, when is the maximum finishing time of a task instance under EDF. The finishing time can then be used to show that the reconfiguration does not postpone the execution of the blocked task for too long.

Lemma 3. *The upper bound of the finishing time of the instance i of task τ_r in configuration $c \in C$ is*

$$f_{r,i} \leq r_{r,i} + T_r * U_p$$

with $U_p = U(c)$ and T_r the period of task τ_r.

6.1. Scheduling of Profile Reconfiguration

Proof. Let t_2 be the deadline of task τ_r ($t_2 = d_{r,i}$), t_1 the release time of τ_r ($t_1 = r_{r,i}$) and let t_0 be the starting time of a task τ_i so that the interval $[t_0, t_2]$ is the longest interval of continuous utilization of tasks (comp. Figure 6.4). Note that t_0 must be the release time of some periodic instance. Let $C_p(t_0, t_2)$ be the total computation time of all instances in the interval $[t_0, t_2]$ with $r_k \geq t_0$ and $d_k \leq t_2$, which can be computed as

$$C_p(t_0, t_2) = \sum_{r_k \geq t_0, d_k \leq t_2} C_k = \sum_{i=1}^{n} \left\lfloor \frac{t_2 - t_0}{T_i} \right\rfloor C_i. \tag{6.8}$$

Now, observe that

$$C_p(t_0, t_2) = \sum_{i=1}^{n} \left\lfloor \frac{t_2 - t_0}{T_i} \right\rfloor C_i \leq \sum_{i=1}^{n} \frac{t_2 - t_0}{T_i} * C_i = (t_2 - t_0) U_p.$$

Therefore

$$C_p(t_0, t_2) \leq (t_2 - t_0) U_p \tag{6.9}$$

The execution of the instance i of task τ_r can only be postponed or interrupted if there exist other instances of other tasks with a smaller deadline than the deadline $d_{r,i}$. Thus, the upper bound for the finishing time of instance i of task τ_r is

$$f_{r,i} \leq t_0 + C_p(t_0, t_2) \stackrel{6.9}{\leq} t_0 + (t_2 - t_0) U_p.$$

For the first task which is executed in the interval $[t_0, f_{r,i}]$ of continuous utilization exist two different cases: It could be the instance i of task τ_r or an instance of another task. In the first case, $t_0 = t_1$ and in the second case $t_0 < t_1$.

Case 1: $t_0 = t_1$

$$f_{r,i} \leq t_0 + (t_2 - t_0) U_p \stackrel{t_0 = t_1}{=} t_1 + (t_2 - t_1) U_p = r_{r,i} + T_r * U_p.$$

Case 2: $t_0 < t_1$

For this case we show that the upper bound for $f_{r,i}$ from case 1 is also an upper bound for case 2, thus:

$$f_{r,i} \leq t_0 + (t_2 - t_0) U_p < r_{r,i} + T_r * U_p$$

We show this by contradiction, thus we assume that

$$t_0 + (t_2 - t_0) U_p \geq r_{r,i} + T_r * U_p.$$

As per definition $r_{r,i} = t_1$ and $T_r = (t_2 - t_1)$. Substituting them yields to

$$t_0 + (t_2 - t_0) U_p \geq t_1 + (t_2 - t_1) U_p.$$

6. The Flexible Resource Manager - Analysis

In the next step the brackets are dissolved:

$$t_0 + t_2 U_p - t_0 U_p \geq t_1 + t_2 U_p - t_1 U_p.$$

Subtracting $t_2 U_p$ and factoring t_0 and t_1 out yields

$$t_0(1 - Up) \geq t_1(1 - Up).$$

Dividing trough $(1 - U_p)$ (which is positive) leads to:

$$t_0 \geq t_1,$$

which is a contradiction. ∎

Part of this proof was inspired by the schedulability proof of EDF as it can be found in [But04, pp.92].

The next theorem is the fundamental theorem, which is used to decide whether the FRM can allow an over-allocation. Thus, for a given plan, which solves a conflict in case of a resource requirement inside of a profile boundary that cannot be fulfilled, the reconfiguration can be feasibly scheduled immediately and atomically.

Theorem 3. *A reconfiguration due to exhaustion at time t_r from configuration c_a to c_b can be atomically, feasibly and immediately scheduled under EDF at any time, if*

$$W_{\text{reconf}}(c_a, c_b) \leq (1 - U_p) T_{min} \qquad (6.10)$$

with $c_a, c_b \in C$, $T_{min} = \min\{T_{\rho_{\tau_i,j}} | \rho_{\tau_i,j} \in c_a\}$, $W_{\text{reconf}}(c_a, c_b)$ the WCET of the reconfiguration and $U_p = \max\{U(c_a), U(c_b)\}$.

Proof. The attributes atomic, feasible, and immediate can be proven with the previous lemmas of this chapter: The reconfiguration is scheduled under EDF using the TBS approach (comp. Section 4.2.2$_{42}$) with the deadline assignment: $d^*_{r,i} = t_r + W_{\text{reconf}} + \lambda$, with $\lambda = \frac{W_{\text{reconf}}}{U_s} - W_{\text{reconf}}$. As EDF/TBS is used, the schedulability criteria is $U_p + U_s \leq 1$, which must be fulfilled to guarantee feasible schedulability for the tasks and the reconfiguration.

Atomic: In Corollary 1$_{70}$ it was shown that the reconfiguration is atomic if $T_i \geq W_{\text{reconf}} + \lambda$ with $\lambda > 0$ holds for all tasks $\tau_i \in \Gamma$. This criteria can be derived from Equation 6.10:

$$W_{\text{reconf}}(c_a, c_b) \leq (1 - U_p) T_{min},$$

with $U_s = 1 - U_p$ as the upper bound for the server utilization the equation can be substituted to:

$$W_{\text{reconf}}(c_a, c_b) \leq U_s T_{min}.$$

6.1. Scheduling of Profile Reconfiguration

As mentioned in the proof of Lemma 2[71] (Equation 6.6[71]) $U_s = \frac{W_{\text{reconf}}(c_a, c_b)}{W_{\text{reconf}}(c_a, c_b) + \lambda}$

$$W_{\text{reconf}}(c_a, c_b) \leq \frac{W_{\text{reconf}}(c_a, c_b)}{W_{\text{reconf}}(c_a, c_b) + \lambda} T_{min}.$$

Solving this equation for T_{min} yields

$$T_{min} \geq W_{\text{reconf}}(c_a, c_b) + \lambda \qquad (6.11)$$

Thus, $T_i \geq W_{\text{reconf}} + \lambda$ with $\lambda > 0$ holds for all tasks $\tau_i \in \Gamma$ as T_{min} is the minimum of all periods.

Feasible: Using Lemma 2[71], the feasibility can be proven. Thus, it must hold that:

$$U_p \leq 1 - \frac{W_{\text{reconf}}(c_a, c_b)}{W_{\text{reconf}}(c_a, c_b) + \lambda}.$$

This criteria can be derived from Equation 6.10[74]:

$$W_{\text{reconf}}(c_a, c_b) \leq (1 - U_p) T_{min}.$$

Dividing the equation through T_{min} and solving this equation for U_p yields to

$$U_p \leq 1 - \frac{W_{\text{reconf}}(c_a, c_b)}{T_{min}}.$$

As consequence from the Condition 6.10[74] in the atomic part of the prove in 6.11 it holds: $T_{min} \geq W_{\text{reconf}}(c_a, c_b) + \lambda$. Thus,

$$U_p \leq 1 - \frac{W_{\text{reconf}}(c_a, c_b)}{W_{\text{reconf}}(c_a, c_b) + \lambda}.$$

Immediate: $\tau_{r,i}$ is the task which causes the conflict by allocating resources in its profile boundaries. It is the task with the shortest deadline; otherwise it would not be executed by EDF. With the proof of the atomic criteria it has been shown that no other task can interrupt the reconfiguration. Thus, no other task (except $\tau_{r,i}$) can have a shorter deadline than the reconfiguration deadline $d_{r,i}^* = t_r + W_{\text{reconf}} + \lambda$ and can be executed prior to the reconfiguration under the EDF scheduling policy. Unfortunately $d_{r,i}^* < d_{r,i}$ does not hold in every case, thus the deadline of $\tau_{r,i}$ could be shorter than the assigned deadline of the reconfiguration. For example, if $U_p = 0.5$ and τ_r is the only task with $C_{\tau_r} = 2$ and $T_{\tau_r} = 4$. With

$$W_{\text{reconf}} \leq (1 - U_p) T_{min}$$

the upper bound for the reconfiguration is

$$W_{\text{reconf}} \leq 0.5 * 4 = 2.$$

A reconfiguration with maximum length would get assigned the deadline

$$d_{r,i}^* = t_r + \frac{W_{\text{reconf}}}{U_s} = t_r + \frac{2}{0.5} = t_r + 4.$$

6. The Flexible Resource Manager - Analysis

If $t_r > r_{r,i}$ the assigned deadline of the reconfiguration is greater than the deadline of $\tau_{r,i}$ in this example. Thus, under EDF $\tau_{r,i}$ would be executed. But the execution of the reconfiguration needs to be immediate, because task $\tau_{r,i}$ is blocked due to new resource requirements. These resources are not present and must be freed by the reconfiguration. The idea is to swap computation time of the reconfiguration with computation time of the task instance $\tau_{r,i}$. To swap the computation time the deadline of the reconfiguration $d^*_{r,i}$ reported to the EDF scheduler can be modified to

$$d^\dagger_{r,i} = t_r + W_{\text{reconf}}.$$

To prove that by this deadline manipulation the EDF scheduler selects the reconfiguration prior to the task instance $\tau_{r,i}$ it has to be shown that $d^\dagger_{r,i} \leq d_{r,i}$ [1]. As the latest moment of reconfiguration t_r could be the last instruction of the task instance $\tau_{r,i}$ the upper bound for the modified deadline is $d^\dagger_{r,i} \leq f_{r,i} + W_{\text{reconf}}$, with $f_{r,i}$ the finishing time of $\tau_{r,i}$ without a reconfiguration. Thus, it has to be shown that

$$f_{r,i} + W_{\text{reconf}} \leq d_{r,i}. \tag{6.12}$$

Additionally it has to be proven that this deadline manipulation does not violate any deadlines. The deadline modification swaps only the computation time between the reconfiguration and the task instance $\tau_{r,i}$, thus the schedulability of other tasks trivially is not violated. But it has to be shown that this exchange of computation time would not violate the deadline of task $\tau_{r,i}$. Task $\tau_{r,i}$ is halted for the reconfiguration time. Thus, the following upper bound for the finishing time of the task instance plus the reconfiguration time must not exceed the deadline of the task instance: $f_{r,i} + W_{\text{reconf}} \leq d_{r,i}$, with $f_{r,i}$ the finishing time of $\tau_{r,i}$ without a reconfiguration. This is the same equation as Equation 6.12. Thus, proving this equation proves that the reconfiguration is immediately executed and the swap of execution time between task $\tau_{r,i}$ and the reconfiguration process does not violate the feasible schedule.

Using Lemma 3_{72} the upper bound for finishing time of $\tau_{r,i}$ with an interruption of an atomic and immediately scheduled reconfiguration due to exhaustion is:

$$f_{r,i} + W_{\text{reconf}} \leq r_{r,i} + T_r U_p + W_{\text{reconf}}$$

As condition is $W_{\text{reconf}} \leq (1 - U_p)T_{min}$, the inequation can be written as:

$$f_{r,i} + W_{\text{reconf}} \leq r_{r,i} + T_r U_p + (1 - U_p)T_{min}.$$

As $T_r \geq T_{min}$ holds:

$$f_{r,i} + W_{\text{reconf}} \leq r_{r,i} + T_r U_p + (1 - U_p)T_r.$$

---
[1] In the case of $d^\dagger_{r,i} = d_{r,i}$ it is assumed that the EDF scheduler prefers the reconfiguration

Factoring out leads to:
$$f_{r,i} + W_{\text{reconf}} \leq r_{r,i} + T_r.$$
As period is equal to deadline $r_{r,i} + T_r = d_{r,i}$, thus
$$f_{r,i} + W_{\text{reconf}} \leq d_{r,i}$$
which was to be shown. Thus, immediate execution of the reconfiguration leads to a feasible schedule.
∎

With Theorem 3[74] exists an upper bound for the reconfiguration time $W_{\text{reconf}}(c_a, c_b)$. This upper bound depends only on the utilization of the application tasks U_p of the two configurations c_a, c_b and the minimal period of these tasks T_{min}. Both values (U_p and T_{min}) are known for any two given configurations and the reconfiguration between them. Also, the reconfiguration time $W_{\text{reconf}}(c_a, c_b)$ is known, namely it is the sum of all WCETs of enter- and leave-functions which have to be executed due to profile reconfiguration. Thus, the FRM can decide whether a reconfiguration is atomically, feasibly and immediately schedulable. When the FRM tries to find a plan to solve a conflict before activating an over-allocated configuration Theorem 3[74] delivers the criteria to be checked.

Figure 6.5[78] illustrates the relation of Equation 6.10[74] for four different processor utilizations U_p ranging from 60 % to 90 %. Assume that reconfiguration has a WCET of 800 µs. In order to guarantee the schedulability for a task set that may utilize the processor up to 90 %, the minimum period of all tasks must not fall below 8,000 µs. In contrast, if a utilization of 60 % suffices, the minimum period can be reduced to 2,000 µs.

Theorem 3[74] defines the upper bound for the reconfiguration time to
$$W_{\text{reconf}}(c_a, c_b) \leq (1 - U_p)T_{min},$$
thus W_{reconf} has to be lower than T_{min} as it holds $0 \leq U_p \leq 1$. If T_{min} is very low this could lead to a problem if reconfiguration times are higher. To deal with this problem another boundary T^*_{min} can be used in the formula of Theorem 3[74] for T_{min}, when task instances of applications can be left out. This is the case if the applications have specified an omit factor in their corresponding profiles. Thus, T^*_{min} can be used to calculate the upper bound for the reconfiguration time defined as follows:
$$T^*_{min} = \min\left\{T_{\rho_{\tau_i,j}} * o(\rho_{\tau_i,j}) | \rho_{\tau_i,j} \in \{c_a, c_b\}\right\}.$$

6.2. Analysis for Deadlock Freeness

If a resource manager reassigns multiple resources at run-time, as the FRM does, the assignment has to be free from deadlocks. Especially in the context of hard-real time mechatronic systems, where a

6. The Flexible Resource Manager - Analysis

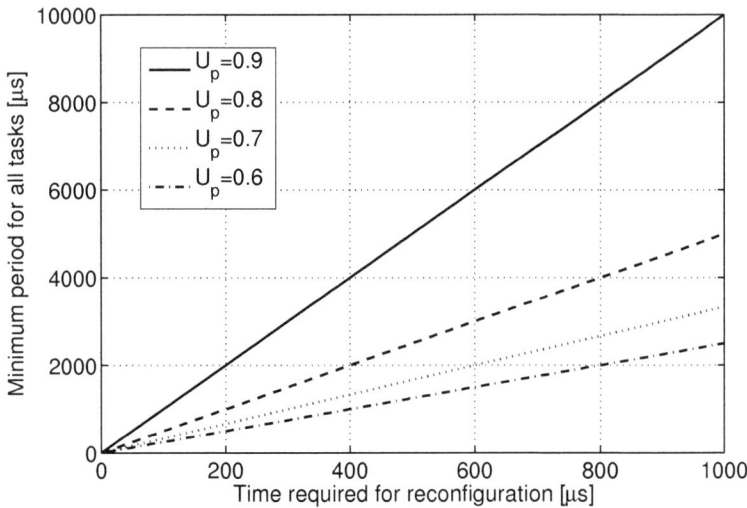

Figure 6.5.: The figure shows the minimum task period required in relation to the reconfiguration time $W_{\text{reconf}} \in [0, 1000]$ for the schedule to be feasible. Four different plots are shown covering processor utilizations from 60 % to 90 %.

deadlock and thus a miss of a deadline has catastrophic consequences.

Conditions for a Deadlock to Exist

The conditions under which a deadlock can arise have been well researched.

Theorem 4. *A deadlock can only arise if all following four conditions are true:*

1. **mutual exclusion condition:** *Tasks claim exclusive control of the resources they require.*

2. **hold while wait condition:** *Tasks hold resources already allocated to them while waiting for additional resources.*

3. **no preemption condition:** *Resources cannot be forcibly removed from the tasks holding them until the resources are used to completion.*

4. **circular wait condition:** *A circular chain of tasks exists, so that each task holds one or more resources that are being requested by the next task in the chain.*

6.2. Analysis for Deadlock Freeness

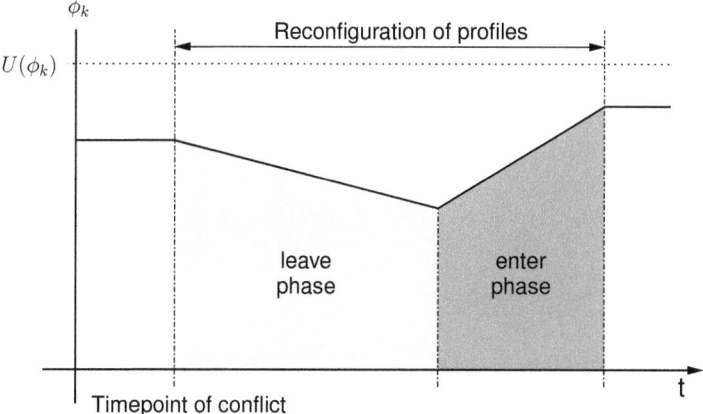

Figure 6.6.: Utilization profile during reconfiguration

Proof. A proof has been presented by COFFMAN ET AL. in [CES71]. ∎

Deadlocks and the FRM

The following theorem and its proof certify the deadlock freeness of the FRM approach:

Theorem 5. *Allocation by the FRM is deadlock free.*

Proof. To prove that the resource assignment of the FRM is free of deadlocks, it has to be shown that the three states the system can be in are free of deadlocks: guaranteed state, over-allocated state and the reconfiguration of configurations.

Guaranteed state: In a guaranteed allocation state all resources can be granted at once, thus no task has to wait for a resource assigned to another task. This means that the *circular wait condition* is not true, thus no deadlock can arise.

Over-allocated configurations: In an over-allocation state a resource conflict is solved immediately by executing the plan to solve the conflict, thus by forcing the system into another profile configuration. This breaks the *hold while wait condition* and/or the *no preemption condition*. The hold while wait for condition is left if the plan forbids the allocation of the task raising the conflict by forcing this task to a profile with lower resource requirements. In the case that the plan allot to force other tasks to a profile with lower resource requirements the *no preemption condition* is not true.

6. The Flexible Resource Manager - Analysis

Reconfiguration of configurations: In the first phase of profile reconfiguration only the leave functions of the profiles, which are changed, are executed. In this phase only resources are allowed to be released, not to be allocated. Only in the second phase, where the enter methods are executed, resources can be allocated again (comp. Figure 6.6). If the plan allot to reconfigure to guaranteed allocation no other conflict can arise. If the plan allots a reconfiguration to another over-allocated configuration another conflict can arise, for which also a plan exists. As reconfiguration or sequence of reconfigurations is atomic, no deadlock can arise in this situation. ∎

6.3. Chapter Conclusion

In this chapter the two characteristics schedulability of resource reconfiguration and deadlock freeness are proved for the FRM. Without the proved theorems of this chapter over-allocation of resources would be impossible in hard real-time systems. In the schedulability section a criterion for the different resource states and profile reconfigurations is analyzed. Criteria for the different states and reconfiguration situations are developed. Especially, for reconfiguration due to exhaustion this leads to Theorem 3_{74}, which describes the criteria for allowing the system to be in an over-allocated state. The criteria guarantee a profile reconfiguration due to exhaustion to be atomically and immediately executed, without violating deadlines of any task. Thus, the requirements of self-optimizing applications for support of dynamic hard real-time resource management is achieved (comp. Section $3.9.1_{33}$).

7. The Flexible Resource Manager - Optimization

The optimization component of the FRM has the objective to maximize the system quality. Thus, it has to find a good profile configuration for the current situation (actual resource allocation within the active profiles) and in case of an over-allocated configuration at least one plan for solving a potential resource conflict. Of course, finding the optimal configuration is an NP-hard problem. Elsewhere, the search for a better configuration is done in the idle time of the applications only under soft real-time constraints. So the worst-case – if no better solution is found – is as bad as if the FRM would not be used. The problem is finding a good heuristic for optimizing the profile configurations during run-time. The heuristic itself should not require too many resources – because it should optimize the resource usage and not utilize to much resources itself. Additionally, a high amicability of the optimization is desired. For the flexibility the optimization algorithm in the FRM framework is exchangeable.

A problem class similar to the planning decisions of the FRM is the page replacement policy in virtual memory systems. BELADY has shown in [Bel66] that the optimal page replacement strategy uses information about the future. The FRM is gathering additional information about the resource requirements of applications compared to classical resource managers. This enables a better planning of which task assigns (unused) resources and when. To avoid profile reconfiguration – for example due to rapid changing resource requirements within one profile of a task – the likeliness of the change of resource requirements and the likeliness of the amount of resources used within a profile are of interest for planning/optimizing the resource assignment. With such information too frequent cyclic reconfiguration can be avoided. Thus, the FRM uses the likeliness as an approximation of the future. The problem is how can a good approximation of the likeliness of the change and the probability of the amount of resources be calculated during run-time.

In this chapter first a mechanism is presented to solve the problem of event prediction (Section 7.1$_{82}$) and after that algorithms are presented to solve the problem of optimizing the profile configurations (Section 7.2$_{87}$).

7. The Flexible Resource Manager - Optimization

7.1. Event Prediction

It is useful to distinguish between different aspects for the likeliness of events in the FRM model: First the allocation situation within the different application profiles is uncertain within the range of the specified resource boundaries and second the mean time between resource allocations of the applications within their profiles is uncertain. What is known with certainty is the current and past resource requirements and system configuration.

In this section it is introduced how the probabilities of the allocation level within the different application profiles and the mean time between resource allocations are acquired by systematic modeling and machine learning techniques. First Bayesian Networks are introduced and it is shown how the probabilities can be modeled with this technique. After that it is briefly discussed what standard methods for Bayesian networks are applied to learn the probabilities by means of the model.

Modeling the Probabilities

The determination of occurrence probabilities should include all available information about the occurrence. For the FRM approach, this information includes at least the current allocation of resources and the current configuration of the system. More information may be provided by the applications. For example, behold an engine control in a car. The required resource CPU utilization of the controller is depending on the current number of revolutions of the engine. This information should be modeled as random variables, which influence the probability of the required CPU utilization of the controller. Generalized, the general problem is to model a joint probability of several random variables, e.g. the allocation of resources and application specific variables.

With so-called Bayesian Networks joint probabilities can be modeled and calculated [Pea88]. Bayes' theorem allows more precise calculation of a posteriori probability distribution on the basis of former a priori probabilities, when some additional knowledge about the world is given. Thus, this approach offers a method to model and calculate the needed probabilities for the FRM.

In the domain of Bayesian Networks the knowledge about the world is referred to as evidence. Hard and soft evidence are distinguished, where hard evidence denotes a fact that is known for sure and soft evidence means that an a posteriori probability for the fact is available. A Bayesian Network is a directed, acyclic graph (V, G) with nodes $v \in V$ and directed edges $e \in G$. Nodes represent discrete or continuous variables. A directed edge $e \in G$ from node X_i to node X_j denotes that variable X_j depends on X_i (comp. Figure 7.1[83]). This dependency is quantified by the conditional probability distribution $P(X_i|Parents(X_i))$ for each node in the network [Cha91].

A special kind of Bayesian Networks are so called Dynamic Bayesian Networks (DBN) [Mur02].

7.1. Event Prediction

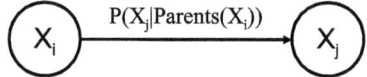

Figure 7.1.: A simple Bayesian Network.

While conventional Bayesian Networks provide a probabilistic model for static states, DBNs explicitly model time and give an alternative representation for Markov processes. DBNs model time as time slices and assume that each time slice contains a number of non-observable variables X_i and a number of observable variables E_t (comp. Figure 7.2$_{83}$).

A process, spanning over a number of time slices, is called a Markov process, when the state of the current time slice depends only on a finite number of predecessor time slices. The Markov property avoids the need for consideration of an infinite number of predecessor time slices. First order MP can be described by an initial distribution $P(X_0)$ and a transition probability $P(X_{t+1}|X_t)$. The concept of DBN extends Markov processes by a sensor model $P(E_t|X_t)$ (comp. again Figure 7.2). The sensor model is the connection between the non-observable variables X_t and the observable variables E_t.

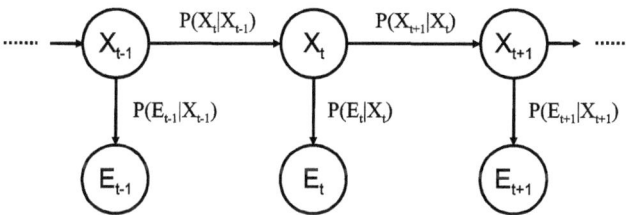

Figure 7.2.: A simple Dynamic Bayesian Network.

Four kinds of inference in DBN can be distinguished: filtering (calculation of the current belief state for X_t), forecasting (calculation of a future state), smoothing (calculation of a distribution of former time slice $k : X_k|e_{1:t}, 1 < k < t$), and finding the most likely sequence of states, which leads to the current state. For planning and scheduling problems, filtering and forecasting are most relevant, since filtering determines the belief state of the current situation while forecasting estimates the future development of the DBN. Thus, the combination of the two inference processes can enable an estimation based on current knowledge.

In order to use DBN for the FRM approach to determine occurrence probability of resource requests, the process of changing resource allocation has to be modeled in interdependent time slices.

7. The Flexible Resource Manager - Optimization

In order to accelerate the inference process and the learning process (see next section), small models are desirable. Thus, each resource variable is modeled separately for each profile. The resource allocation for each resource ϕ_k is modeled as discrete random variable, which is defined by an ordered set $\phi_{k,1} = \phi_{k,\min}, ..., \phi_{k,l} = \phi_{k,\max} \in [\phi_{k,\min}, \phi_{k,\max}]$, with $l \in \mathbb{N}$. This means that in this model the application amount of resource which is allocated depends on this discrete values. As the steps of this values are coarser than the real allocation units, the number of resource states is smaller than in the FRM approach. This abstraction helps to keep the models small. A resource request, which fits not exactly onto a discrete resource variable, is round up to the next discrete resource variable. If the task has specified in the profile discrete steps for the resource ϕ_k (comp. Section 5.2.1$_{53}$ Resource Requirements) these steps are used to build the ordered set. For example, an application has knowledge that in a profile its memory consumption is only exact 128kb, 256kb or 512kb of memory. In this case the ordered set would be: $\phi_{mem,1} = 128kb, \phi_{mem,2} = 256kb, \phi_{mem,3} = 512kb$. If the steps are not specified in the profile by an application the set is built equidistantly.

In the simplest case a DBN modeling the processes of changing allocations contains only the resource requests as a single variable. Figure 7.3$_{85}$a shows an example DBN using only a single variable. The discrete random variable R represents the resource. The variable can have the values of the ordered set. Using the previous introduced example again, R_t would represent the memory consumption at time t and could have one of the three values: 128kb, 256kb or 512kb. In this model the probability of the resource request depends only on resource consumption of the previous time slices (e.g. $P(R_{t+1}|R_t)$). This is denoted by the edge from R_{t-1} to R_t respectively R_t to R_{t+1}.

If application specific information about the effect of environmental variables on the resource is available in the profile, they can be included as sensor model. Figure 7.3$_{85}$b shows an example DBN with two application specific variables A_1 and A_2. In this example, the probability of the resource requirements depends in each time slice directly only on the environmental variables. This is denoted by the fact that in each time slice t the variable R_t has only incoming edges from the specific variables $A_{1,t}$ and $A_{2,t}$. These edges represent the probabilities $P(R_i|A_{1,t})$ and $P(R_i|A_{2,t})$. From one time slice to another only the probabilities between the environmental variables are modeled (e.g. $P(A_{1,t}|A_{1,t-1})$). Looking again at the previous example, the application has only three levels of memory consumption (128kb, 256kb or 512kb). The application could be a feedback controller with three different control strategies each requiring one of the levels of memory consumption. The selection of the control strategies depends only on the extern must value for the controller and a read sensor value. The must value is represented in the DBN model as variable A_1 and the sensor value as A_2. However, the emerging overhead has to be balanced against the more accurate probabilities.

With the model of DBN it is also possible to calculate the occurrence probability of change events in every time slice. The occurrence probability can be calculated for every possible event – not only

84

7.1. Event Prediction

for the amount of resource requirements – in a fixed planning horizon.

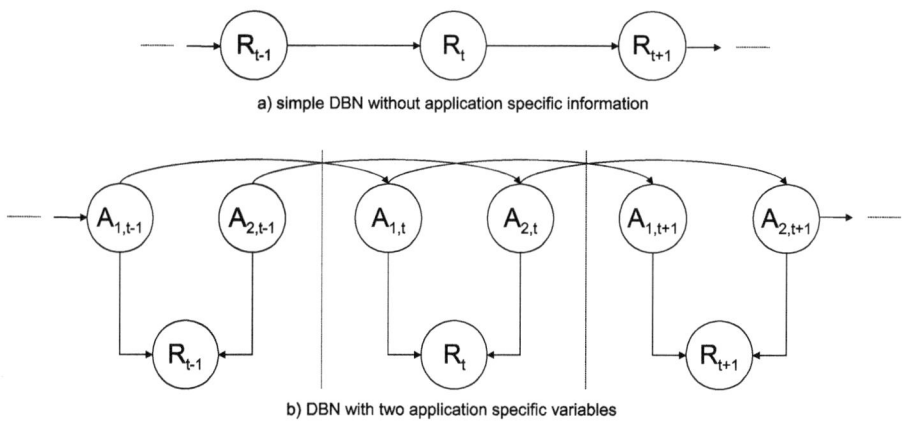

Figure 7.3.: Using Dynamic Bayesian Networks (DBN) to model resource allocation.

Learning the Probabilities

In the previous section the general structure of DBNs was defined, which is used to estimate the occurrence probability of future resource requirements or other events. This structure is either very simple - if no application specific information is available - or is easily defined by an application expert. However, the structure is the first step in the definition of Bayesian Networks. The second part is the definition of a conditional probability distribution $P(X_i|Parents(X_i))$ for each node in the network. The conditional probability distributions are usually called the parameters of the network. While the structure definition corresponds nicely with causal thinking of human experts and thus is easily performed, the definition of the parameters is a much harder task. If the expert fails to give appropriate estimations of the parameters, the quality of the prediction is poor. Thus, alternative methods for the determination of the required conditional probability distributions are desirable. Machine learning offers such alternatives by learning the conditional probability distributions. The local probability distributions are very similar to probabilistic classification problems - given an individual defined by several criteria (the characteristics of the parents) the probability distribution that the individual belongs to certain classes (the characteristics of the child) are given. Thus, Bayesian Networks can be viewed as sets of probabilistic classification/regression models [Hec95, Nea03].

7. The Flexible Resource Manager - Optimization

Probabilistic classification is the generic term for machine learning techniques in which individual items are placed into groups based on quantitative information. In the case of Bayesian Networks the probabilistic classification is based on applying Bayes' theorem with strong (naive) independence assumptions. Looking at the example in Figure 7.3b this independence is modeled in the way that resource consumption R_t in each time slice t only depends on the application specific variables A_1, t and A_2, t, which are assumed to be completely independent from each other. Regression analysis is the generic term for techniques which model and analyze several variables, when the focus is on the relationship between a dependent variable (R in Figure 7.3b) and one or more independent variables (A_1 and A_2 in Figure 7.3b). More specifically, the regression analysis with Bayesian Networks helps how the resource consumption R changes when any one of the independent application variables A is varied, while the other independent variables are held fixed.

The basic idea of the learning approach is to use an extended Bayesian Network, a so called augmented network that embeds the original Bayesian Networks. In an augmented network a new kind of nodes, representing the possible relative frequencies of the random variables, is introduced. For each combination of the characteristics of the parents of a node, one frequency node is added to this node in the original network. These nodes are roots in the network and are limited to a single child. Through this approach it is possible to include expert estimations about the parameters. The expert estimations are given in the profile in the form of a probability mass function $F\rho_{\tau_i,j}, \phi_k(x)$ (comp. Section 5.2.1$_{53}$ Resource Requirements). If no estimation is specified as starting point for the learning process an equal distribution has to be used. The learning process approaches the true distribution faster, if the expert estimation is closer to the real distribution than the equal distribution. Thus, the learning process is only used to refine the expert estimation and an optimization algorithm can immediately benefit from prediction of events.

Bayes' theorem is used to calculate the a posteriori distributions for the frequency distributions given a sample of observations regarding the original network. To estimate the parameters of the nodes in the original network the statistical method *Maximum likelihood estimation (MLE)* is used. For a fixed set of observations for the variables of the underlying probability model, the maximum likelihood estimation picks the values of the model parameters that make the observations *more likely* than any other values of the parameters would make them. The parameters of the nodes in the original networks are then the expected values of the probability distribution of the relative frequencies. Thus, this learning approach can be used to improve an expert estimation of the parameters of the Bayesian Network. The advantage of this approach is that the accuracy of the expert estimations is improved during run-time. The expert estimation is only used as an initial estimation. Thus, even when the expert estimation is not good the real probability distribution is approximated during run-time. Also if the real probability distribution is changing over time – e.g. due to environmental changes – this approach adapts the computed probability distributions during run-time.

The FRM provides the samples for the learning process. This process and the inference procedure to determine the occurrence probabilities are performed in idle time. The occurrence probabilities of events are finally provided in a look-up table. Thus, to choose an appropriate granularity of the probabilistic model is a critical point. If the probabilistic model is not fine enough, the approach will not be able to provide useful probabilities. On the other hand, the size of the look-up table and the look-up time grow exponentially with some extensions of the model.

Evaluation

In Chapter 11_{129} the benefit of the event prediction is shown in simulation. Without using event prediction the FRM more often activates over-allocated configurations which have to be left short after activation. This leads into a higher reconfiguration overhead.

7.2. Finding a Good Profile Configuration

Optimal assignment of resources is a challenging task. The Flexible Resource Manager must be capable of determining and activating a configuration, which has a good quality and efficiently utilizes the system resources during run-time. In general this problem is NP-hard. Furthermore, the resource management is subject to various stochastic events caused by the interactions between the applications and their environment. Examples of events include allocating/de-allocating resources, adding/deleting profiles and adding/deleting applications. The system must be capable of adapting its behaviour according to these disturbances. Finding an appropriate reaction for some event is also an NP-hard problem.

With this in mind, the FRM was designed in such a way, that finding a good or the optimal configuration does not need to take place under hard real-time constrains. As described before, an over-allocation is only activated when a *plan back* has been found. This allows the application of heuristics, which perhaps find a better, but not the optimal configuration and it has no catastrophic effects on the application if finding a better configuration takes longer than expected. As calculation of the FRM is done in the idle task, it is to mention that in the worst case the system quality is as bad as if no FRM would be used, except of the memory used by the FRM.

Using stochastic information

Besides finding a better configuration another important ability of the optimization algorithm is to detect whether the overhead of a reconfiguration to an over-allocation is higher than the benefit. Thus,

7. The Flexible Resource Manager - Optimization

a good configuration is not always the configuration with the highest quality value. The next two examples clarify this problem. If a configuration with a high quality value is left, due to resource conflict every time it is activated, an immediately activation does not make sense. If an application frees resources only for a short period of time and reallocates the resources again, it does not make sense to put these resources at other applications' disposal. On that score the probabilistic analysis can be used to determine and update the mean time of resource changes in resource allocation per profile at run-time, as described in Section 7.1_{82}. Thus, the mean time is modeled as a random variable in a DBN. The application can specify a mean time, if it has information about its future resource requirements in detail. This information is used as an expert estimation and improved during run-time. With this mean time the algorithm can assess whether the overhead is justifiable to put the released resources to other applications' disposal. Restricting the information about the minimum and maximum amount of resources specified in the profiles can lead to poor results. In Chapter 11_{129} experiments are presented, in which it is shown that this information is not sufficient to decide which over-allocated configuration to activate in future. Especially, when switching some application into new profiles it is not clear how many resources this new profile would allocate inside its minimum/maximum resource boundaries. Planning with the minimum resource boundary could lead into needless reconfiguration when the application quickly allocates more resources and a reconfiguration back due to an over-allocation conflict is required. If planning with the maximum resource boundary of the profiles from every task, no over-allocation would be possible at all.

Thus, the optimization algorithm can plan much better, when using the probabilistic information for resource assignment. On the one hand, possible resource consumption inside the profiles' resource boundaries can be specified. On the other hand, information about resource allocation is gathered by the event prediction module while the profile is active. To shrink the possible search, space for the optimization of the range of resource consumption is segmented into a fixed number of discrete values. These values are then associated with probabilities of the resource allocation. The associated probabilities can then be used by the planning algorithm to activate an over-allocation configuration with a high quality and a lower chance that a conflict occurs due to over-allocation in the near future.

In the following two different optimization algorithms are introduced, which have been implemented. An evaluation of the algorithms is presented in Chapter 11_{129}.

Optimization algorithms

For test purpose and proof of concept of the approach two simple optimization strategies were developed. The methods are referred to as the complete method and the simple greedy method.

Complete

The *complete method* builds the complete profile configuration graph in memory. Thus, it can find the best configuration for the current situation, by examining all possible configurations and calculating the quality for each possible, feasible and (from the current configuration) reachable configuration. Of course this method is only suitable for a small number of applications and profiles. As the number of configurations grows with the number of applications and profiles this method requires much memory and is not suitable for embedded controller. The purpose of this method is to have a reference, which can be used for the other algorithms for comparison. Two different characteristics of this algorithm have been implemented, one of them uses stochastic information and the other one does not.

Simple Greedy

This algorithm uses a simple strategy. In the first phase a restricted breadth first search is used to explore the neighborhood of one configuration to look for a better configuration with only a little change of application profiles. The algorithm is focused on a small memory usage, thus only a better configuration is saved. If the current resource consumption is not changing, the range of the breadth first search is increased to find a better configuration outside the neighborhood of the current configuration. This avoids the algorithm to stuck in local maxima. If a better over-allocation configuration is found in the neighborhood of the current configuration a way back to a guaranteed configuration is searched (for the plan to solve a conflict) also with a breadth first search. If no guaranteed configuration can be found within the boundary of the breadth first search the boundary of the neighborhood to be searched in is increased. Like the complete method this algorithm is implemented in two versions: With the use of stochastic information and without it. Some parameters of the algorithm can be changed during run-time and are evaluated later in this thesis (Chapter 11_{129}). For example, the depth of the breadth first search can be changed after the FRM activates the best found configuration. Also, the threshold can be changed from which a configuration with a better quality is rejected for activation due to probabilistic information about a possible future conflict. In the evaluation the algorithms are compared against the complete method according to quality, the use of probabilistic information about the future and their resource usage.

7.3. Chapter Conclusion

In this chapter the optimization algorithms for the FRM were briefly presented, which evaluation is presented in Chapter 11_{129}. In the section event prediction the likeliness of resource changes and amount of resource consumption inside the profile boundaries are estimated with the help of Dynamic

7. The Flexible Resource Manager - Optimization

Bayesian Networks. With this additional approximation of the future the planning and optimization algorithm has a better foundation to develop strategies for future events and to decide if it is useful to activate a specific over-allocated configuration or not. In the second section the different optimization algorithms are presented. Simple strategies for test purpose and the look-ahead optimization are introduced, which utilizes game-theocratical methods. Together with the two previous chapters this completes the FRM concept, correctness (schedulable and deadlockfree) and optimization.

8. Building a Self-Optimizing RTOS

If self-optimizing applications change their behavior and their resource requests dynamically during run-time, then also the underlying RTOS should reconfigure its QoS by means of the currently provided services. For example, a specific protocol stack should only be present in the RTOS, when applications request this protocol for their communication. I.e., a reconfigurable/customizable RTOS includes only those services that are currently required by its applications. Hence, services of the RTOS must be loaded or removed on demand. Thus, the RTOS also releases valuable resources that can be used by applications.

As self-optimizing applications are – in the context of this thesis – embedded mechatronic systems, they run under hard or soft real-time constraints. Thus, the reconfiguration of RTOS components is critical. The RTOS always has to assure a timely and functional correct behavior and has to support the required services. Hence, the reconfiguration underlies the same deadlines as the normal operation of the applications. To handle exactly this problem, the *Profile Framework* and *Flexible Resource Manager* can be applied to the RTOS as well. The FRM model executes the reconfiguration under real-time constrains. The acceptance test inside the FRM assures that the reconfiguration does not violate real-time constraints.

The main idea is to release resources of system services by deactivating, activating basic versions or activating development alternatives (e.g. an implementation on the FPGA instead on the CPU) of these services. These different states of the services are modeled as different profiles for each service. Then, these RTOS components will be handled by the FRM as normal application profiles. Thus, no change of the FRM model is required. For this purpose an extension of the offline configurator TEReCS for the online case is presented in this chapter.

First, in Section 8.1, the operating system DREAMS and its offline configurator TEReCS, developed by DIETZE and BÖKE, are presented. They are used as a basis to build a self-optimizing RTOS. In Section 8.2_{94} the extension to the online case of the configurator TEReCS will be presented. Then Section 8.3_{97} describes the combination of this new online capable configurator and the *Flexible Resource Management*. The section also treats the integration into the RTOS. Concluding, a case study of the approach is presented in Section 8.4_{101}.

8. Building a Self-Optimizing RTOS

8.1. The RTOS DREAMS

Operating systems and run-time platforms for even heterogeneous processor architectures can be constructed from customizable components (*skeletons*) out of the DREAMS's (**D**istributed **R**eal-time **E**xtensible **A**pplication **M**anagement **S**ystem) library [Dit95, Dit99, DB98]. By creating a configuration description all desired objects of the system have to be interconnected and afterwards in a fine-grained manner customized. The primary goal of that process is to include only such components and properties that are really required by the application.

8.1.1. TEReCS

The creation of a final configuration description for DREAMS was automated during the project TEReCS (**T**ools for **E**mbedded **R**eal-Time **C**ommunication **S**ystems) [Bök99, Bök03] funded by the DFG [1]. During that project a methodology was developed in order to synthesize and configure the operating system for distributed embedded applications.

TEReCS strictly distinguishes between knowledge about the application and expert knowledge about the customizable operating system. Knowledge about the application is considered as a requirement specification. This requirement specification is an input to the configurator. The requirement specification abstractly describes the behavior of the application and some constraints (deadlines), which have to be assured. The behavior of the application is defined by the operating system calls it requests. It specifies which process calls which primitive at what time. Especially the communication channels between the processes have to be specified including their properties (max. data size, period, etc.).

The complete and valid design space of the customizable operating system is specified by a so-called AND/OR service dependency graph in a knowledge base [CBR02]. This domain knowledge contains options, costs, and constraints and defines an over-specification by containing alternative options. The configuration process removes some domain specific knowledge by exploiting knowledge about the application. Thereby, a configuration for the run-time platform will be generated. The integration of the domain and application knowledge defines a knowledge transfer from the application down to the operating system.

The complete valid design space of the configurable operating system is specified by an AND/OR graph:

- Nodes represent *services* of the operating system and are the smallest atomic items, which are subject of the configuration

---

[1] Deutsche Forschungsgemeinschaft (German Research Foundation)

8.1. The RTOS DREAMS

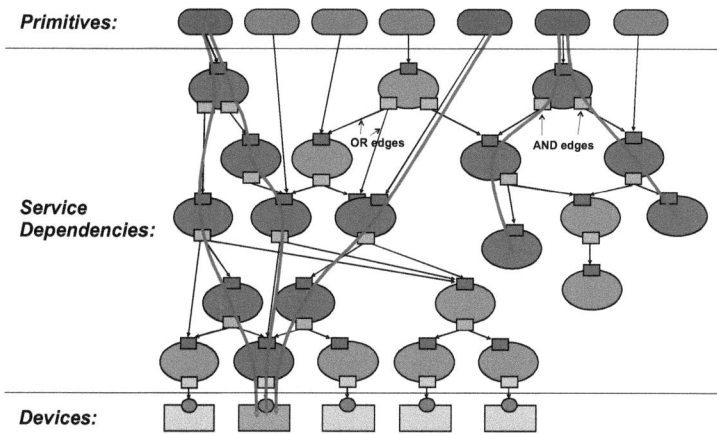

Figure 8.1.: TEReCS's design space description from system primitives via services down to hardware devices (from [Bök03]).

- Mandatory dependencies between services are specified by the AND edges
- Optional or alternative dependencies between services are specified by the OR edges
- Services and their dependencies have costs and can be prioritized
- *Constraints* (preferences, prohibitions, enforcements under specific conditions) for the alternatives can be specified
- Root nodes of the graph are interpreted as *system primitives/system calls* of the operating system

The main objective of the configuration process is to remove all OR dependencies from the graph (over specification → complete and non-ambiguous specification). The configuration can be interpreted as a sub-graph without any alternatives.

The *system primitives* are the root nodes of the service dependency graph. Each of these primitives points to one concrete service. The service dependencies span a complete graph. The leaf nodes can refer to hardware devices. These devices are communication devices, which again refer to communication media.

The algorithm works, e.g. for communication primitives, as follows: A path can be found through the complete graph from the sending primitive down to the sending device, considering the routing and then up to the receiving primitive. The services that are visited on this path have to be installed on

8. Building a Self-Optimizing RTOS

the appropriate nodes of the service platform (see bold nodes in Fig. 8.1). Thereby, the path should create minimal costs by the use of the services.

Such paths will be searched for all primitives that are used in the requirement specification. Because only a subset of all primitives is normally used, especially the particular selection is responsible for the instantiated services and its parameterization. The primitives can be considered as the strings of a puppet. Depending on which strings are pulled, the "configuration" of the puppet will change accordingly. The service dependencies can be compared to the joints of the puppet. Therefore, the algorithm is named *"Puppet Configuration"*.

8.2. From Offline TEReCS to Online TEReCS

To build an online configurable RTOS components which can be re-configured (activated, deactivated, etc.) have to be identified during run-time. For this purpose the offline configurator TEReCS is reused. The TEReCS configurator has been developed only for offline configuration of operating systems comprising very fine-grained optional components that are customizable at source code level. After the system configuration is generated and the operating system synthesized the operating system is fixed during run-time.

To integrate the configurator into the operating system for online reconfiguration within this thesis some modifications had to be carried out in TEReCS. In contrast to the offline case, the basic idea is that only coarse-grained components are configured in the online case. Thus, the overall decision space is restricted and the time spent for the selection of the appropriate components and their parameters can be shortened.

The advantage of TEReCS to define a hierarchy on the valid design space [CBR02] made possible the reuse of the configurator approach for the online case. For the online case a hierarchy is defined above the fine-grained design space. This fine-grained design space is the same design space which was used for the offline configuration in the past. The hierarchy leads to coarse-grained clusters of tightly coupled components. In Figure 8.2_{95} an example is shown for the coarse-grained clusters and in Figure 8.3_{96}A the inside of the cluster OS hierarchy is shown, it exists out of a sub graph of the design space used for the offline configuration.

The TEReCS approach supports customization for the offline case in versatile manner: the inheritance, membership and calling dependencies can be configured at source code level for the C++ classes. Changing inheritance and membership dependencies during run-time is a harder task than changing calling dependencies during run-time (e.g. by using pointers). Thus, tightly coupled components form a cluster, when all inheritance and membership relations for the object-oriented design

8.2. From Offline TEReCS to Online TEReCS

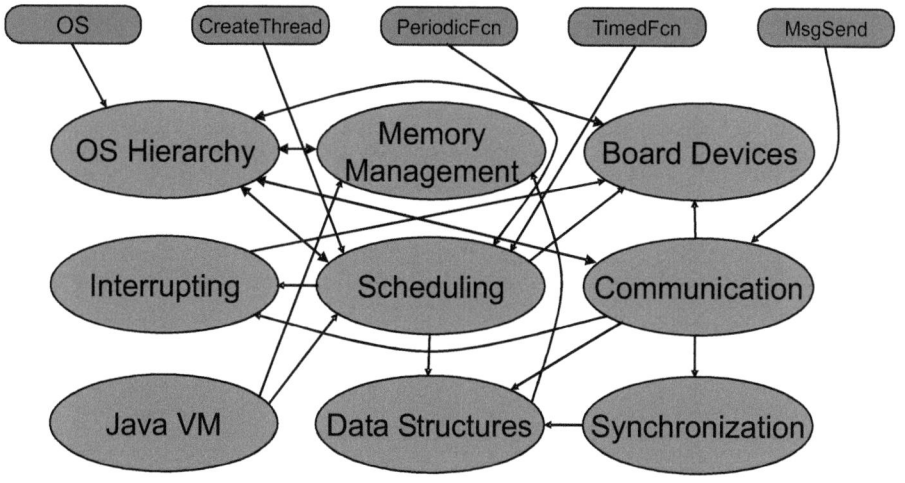

Figure 8.2.: Course-grained OS clusters and their dependencies.

of the RTOS are fixed. Thus, for the online approach the reconfigurations during run-time are limited only to changing the calling dependencies to functions and to instantiate/destroy clusters.

As between clusters only calling dependencies to functions exist, each of these clusters can be – more or less – configured without interference to its neighboring clusters. For the online case the terminology of *internal primitives* is added to the TEReCS approach. The dependencies between the clusters are mapped to these *internal primitives*. These *internal primitives* are primitives which can only be used by other services and not by applications. They are root nodes to the cluster and are triggered/used by other clusters. Thus, independent offline configurations of the clusters are possible for different online use cases. Use cases could be for example: fully used (activated), not used (deceived) or partially used (activated only as a basic version).

The different use cases are different pre-configured solutions, which can be implemented (see Figure 8.3_{96}). Thus, the coarse-grained hierarchy with its pre-defined solutions defines again a valid design space for the TEReCS approach (see Figure 8.4_{97}). The solutions for the clusters made at the fine-grained level become options at the coarse-grained level. Ordinarily due to the hierarchy, the design space at the coarse-grained level is smaller than on the fine-grained level.

The online configuration makes use of pre-defined solutions that have been configured offline. Thus, it is up to the online configuration phase to identify the use cases, for which the solutions have been created and to activate them. The identification is simple, because it depends on the system

8. Building a Self-Optimizing RTOS

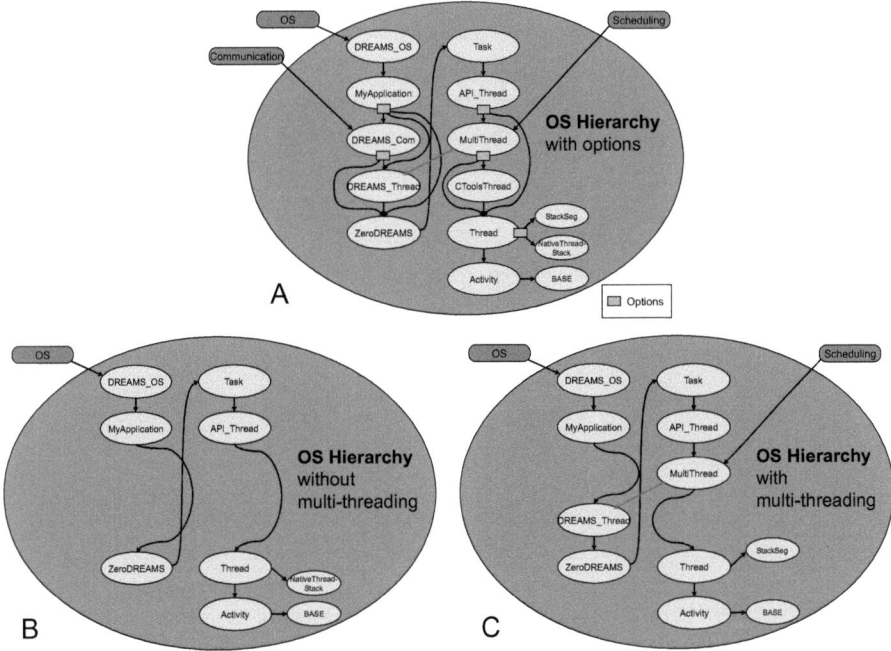

Figure 8.3.: Zoom to the fine-grained level of to the OS cluster with its optional components (A) and two pre-defined configuration examples (B+C).

primitives, which are used by applications and other clusters. Those pre-defined solutions have to be instantiated so that all required primitives are implemented for the concrete situation during run-time. If primitives are unused an alternative cluster can be activated during run-time, which does not implement the unused primitives.

The same system primitives that have been used to create a pre-defined solution are leading to the selection of that solution component in the coarse-grained design space level. This condition must be assured during the specification of the abstract design space for the pre-defined solutions. This problem also must be solved by the system expert offline. This procedure is legal, as TEReCS' main philosophy obliges the encapsulation of all expert knowledge in the design space descriptions.

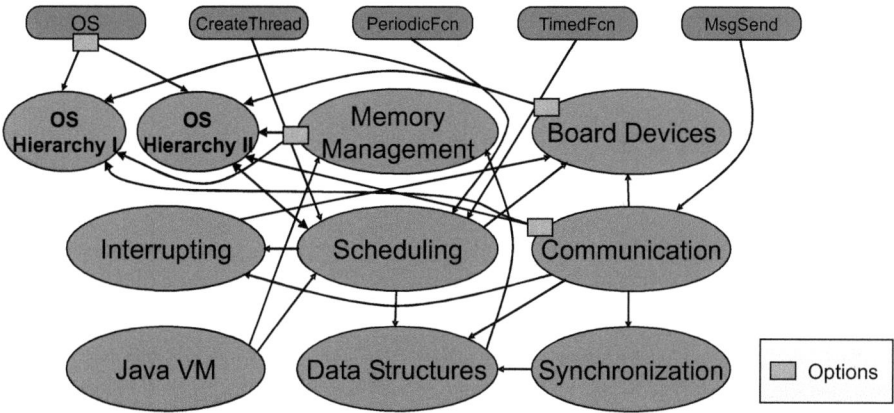

Figure 8.4.: OS design space at 2nd level with integrated options for pre-defined solutions of clusters.

Example

The Figures 8.3 and 8.4$_{97}$ sketch an example for two pre-defined cluster options (B+C). The primitives *Scheduling* and *Communication* in Figure 8.3 are used by the equally named clusters from Figure 8.4$_{97}$. The option B is generated from A if the primitive *Scheduling* is not used. The option C is generated alternatively. In Figure 8.4$_{97}$, the pre-generated solutions B+C are included as the *OS Hierarchy Option I* and *II*. Except the cluster *Scheduling* all other clusters can use both options alternately. Only the cluster *Scheduling* requires explicitly the solution of the *OS Hierarchy II*, which supports multiple threads. If the primitive *CreateThread* will be used, then the cluster *Scheduling* is requested. Thus, the request of the primitive *CreateThread* from an application requests the cluster *Scheduling* to be instantiated. Moreover, as the cluster *Scheduling* requires the internal primitive *Scheduling*, the cluster *OS Hierarchy II* also has to be instantiated instead of the cluster *OS Hierarchy I*.

8.3. Integration of TEReCS and the FRM into the RTOS

In the previous sections the clusters represent the system services, which can be re-configured during-runtime. In this section the FRM approach is employed to mediate the reconfiguration during run-time. As described in the previous chapter, the *Flexible Resource Manager* (FRM) was primary developed to optimize the resource utilization between dynamic applications. Now, resources of RTOS components are additionally considered by modeling them with the profile framework.

8. Building a Self-Optimizing RTOS

The alternatives of the previous section are modeled as different profiles. Using the example of the previous section again, *OS Hierarchy I* and *OS Hierarchy II* are mapped into two profiles of the system service *OS Hierarchy*, which is from the point of view of the FRM handled as a normal application.

For each primitive a new resource is introduced. When an application or other RTOS service wants to use the system primitive, it requests the corresponding resource. Initially, each service holds each corresponding resource of the primitive it provides. When an application or other system service arrives or wants to use a primitive, it has to request the corresponding resource, which must be in the range of the specified resource boundary of its actual profile. As a reaction, the FRM activates a corresponding profile of the service, where the service does not block the primitive by occupying the corresponding resource but implements the primitive by activating an alternative pre-defined solution. The service implements in the enter and leave functions the switch between the pre-defined clusters. These reconfiguration functions are representing the Online-TEReCS module as a whole entity. In a profile the meaning for the system services of holding a primitive they provide is reverse to the meaning of an application: a service holding a primitive means that the primitive is not required and does not need to be implemented. The other way around, when an application holds a primitive, the service has to provide the primitive's code. Instead of modeling, e. g., 10 primitive resources so that they can be requested by 10 applications, the primitive resource has an item counter, as a memory resource has. This item counter tracks the number of distributed primitive assignments to the applications (see Figure 8.6_{100}). This indirect technique allows the FRM controlling when and which alternative option of an RTOS implementation to activate on the base of the current requirements of the applications. This approach also carries out the identification process of the use case of the system service automatically by the FRM. This is the case as the primitives are mapped to resources which are handled by the FRM.

As sketched in Figure 8.5_{99} and before, the reconfiguration of the RTOS cluster components is completely managed by the Online-TEReCS module in the enter/leave functions. The reconfiguration options are modeled as optional profiles that are offered by Online-TEReCS, which are activated and deactivated by the FRM. Each profile defines exactly, which primitives are used by a system service profile and which are not used – as the primitives are modeled as resources. Thus, the FRM does not need to distinguish between the RTOS components and normal applications. The FRM mediates the system primitives (resources) between all the applications and the RTOS. Thus, it handles the competition between the applications and the reconfiguration options of the RTOS. The system primitives represent the dependencies between the services and services block not provided system primitives in corresponding profiles by allocating the system primitive itself. With this two facts the FRM manages and assures that all dependencies are considered during run-time, otherwise the

8.3. Integration of TEReCS and the FRM into the RTOS

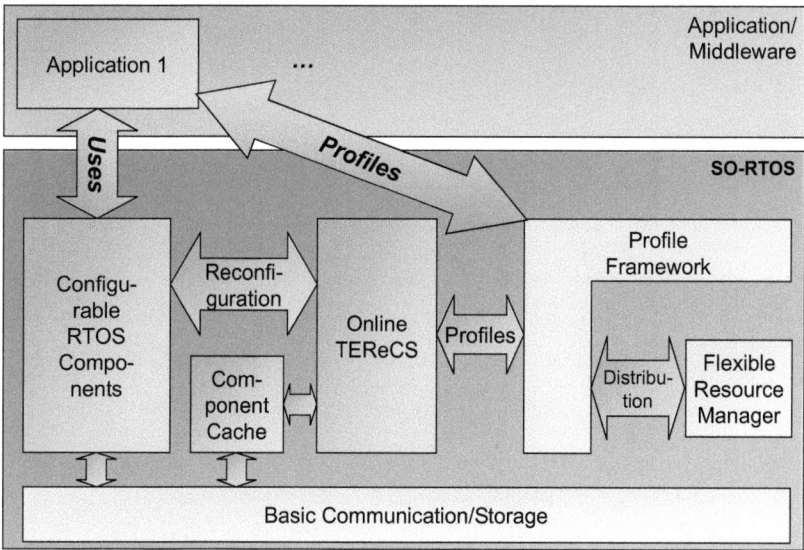

Figure 8.5.: Integration of TEReCS and the FRM framework into the RTOS.

concrete allocation of a system primitive corresponding recourse would by surmount the maximum available number and lead to a infeasible system configuration. Real-time constrains are respected by modeling the reconfiguration time of the RTOS in the switching conditions respectively the minimum dwell time of the profiles and the acceptance test in the FRM.

Applications must define all real-time constrains regarding their future resource allocations. Additionally, an application can only allocate resources in the range of the profile, which is currently active. With this information the FRM guarantees by means of the acceptance test, that all resource allocations can be timely performed. Deactivating a system service, by activating a profile in which this service is not configured into the system, and an application, which is currently not using the service but specifying a possible future use through the defined profile parameters, creates an over-allocation state. The FRM forces a system service only to a deactivated configuration if it can be reactivated "in time" to provide the resources when needed.

The creation of pre-defined solutions for the clusters is done automatically. For each combination of possible requests or dismissals of *system primitives* and *internal primitives* a configuration is generated. For the optimization and the reduction of the design space of the operating system, a system

8. Building a Self-Optimizing RTOS

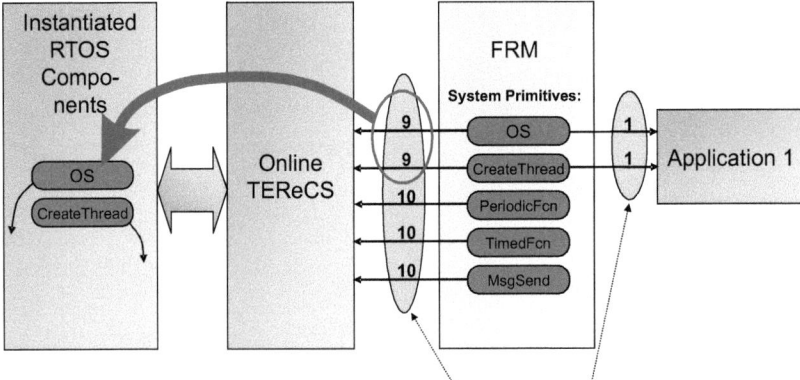

Figure 8.6.: Impact of profile distribution onto the RTOS configuration, where each system primitive can be used by a maximum of 10 applications including the RTOS.

expert might restrict the combinations of parallel instantiated system primitives to only those ones that make sense in a way that they cover other solutions and – with high probability – are not used simultaneously.

A repository stores all pre-defined solutions of the clusters. A cache will temporarily store the code and the description of optional configurations for clusters, in order to speed up the loading of required cluster implementations. The cache can retrieve other configuration's implementations from background storage (hard disk) or from the network (see Figure 8.5_{99}).

The FRM tries to optimize the system according to the current resource requirements of the components (system services and applications) and the quality information of the profiles. To do this, the FRM requests the application and system services to change their current profiles. This results into a reconfiguration of the RTOS and a optimization of the resource usage between the applications and the operating system.

The capabilities for the optimization are exploited by TEReCS during offline generation of the pre-defined cluster configurations for specific use cases. Additionally, the optimization is done always by the FRM based on the respective quality values (see Figure 8.7_{101}).

The FRM approach includes the definition of quality values per profile. Thus, the FRM can not only reason about the optimality of application profiles, but it can additionally reason about the optimality of the RTOS configuration.

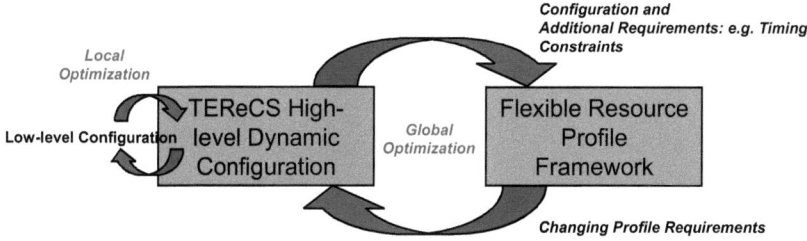

Figure 8.7.: Optimization takes place during offline generation of pre-defined solutions for the clusters and during run-time by the FRM.

8.4. SORTOS - Case Study

The presented approach of a self-optimizing RTOS (SORTOS) – the FRM and the Online-TEReCS component – have been implemented for validation and tested on top of the RTOS DREAMS with an application example from the self-optimizing context.

For the purpose of this case study one system service has been selected: A reconfigurable Ethernet switch [VGPR04].

The bases of the reconfigurable RCOS service are dual-port network nodes that allow setting up line and ring topologies. Each node consists of two external network interfaces that connect the node to its neighbors and an internal interface to an embedded processor. In order to be able to adapt the network nodes to changes in protocols and interface requirements, which cannot be foreseen, reconfigurable hardware for the implementation of the network interfaces is used. On each node one instance of the SO-RTOS with a local FRM is executed.

The nodes handle two different types of data streams: data originating from or terminating at the processor, and streams that are simply passed through. If network traffic is rather small or if real-time requirements are low or even nonexistent, comparatively simple network interfaces are sufficient, which occupy only a few resources. In this case, data packets are forwarded from one port to another by a software implementation on the embedded processor. This causes a high load for the processor, the internal bus and the memory while the FPGA resources can be utilized by other applications. If the software implementation is not able to deliver the required performance, e.g., due to increasing bandwidth or real-time requirements, the two separate interfaces are substituted by a single integrated hardware switch during run-time. This switch is able to forward data packets autonomously and, as a consequence, manages a much higher amount of traffic. However, the structure of this switch is more complex and requires additional FPGA resources, which are no longer available for other

8. Building a Self-Optimizing RTOS

applications. To guarantee real-time constrains in the communication system, bandwidth must be allocated through a bandwidth manager.

The two implementations of the Ethernet switch are selected to build one cluster and are mapped each into one profile. Additionally, a third profile is created, in which the reconfiguration between both switch variants is done. Thus, the implementation to be activated is decided by the FRM. As the node is in a network in which transit traffic goes through the Ethernet switch component it cannot be disabled completely. In Table 8.1 the defined settings of the three profiles are shown.

System service or application	Imp.	Profile								min. dwell time
				Resource requirements				WCET		
		Profile name	Profile quality	FPGA in Slices	Delay	Bandwidth MBit/s	Delay	Enter	Leave	
Ethernet switch	0.0	SW	0	1981	0 ms	86	0 ms	1 ms	1 ms	-
		HW	0	4573	0 ms	0	0 ms	1 ms	1 ms	-
		reconf.	0	1981-6554	10 ms	0-86	0 ms	1 ms	1 ms	10 ms
BW manager	1.0	standard	0	0	0 ms	1-100	20 ms	1 ms	1 ms	-
Self-opt. application	1.0	normal	0	0	0 ms	0	0 ms	1 ms	1 ms	-
		accel.	10	0-3000	10 ms	0	0 ms	1 ms	1 ms	-

Table 8.1.: The profiles of the example scenario.

The first profile includes the software switch, while the second profile includes the hardware switch. Handing over the communication service without packet loss from the software switch to the hardware switch requires a coexistence of both switch implementations. In the short period of reconfiguration the third profile provides the FPGA resources that are necessary for both switch implementations. Thus, no direct connection between the first and the second profile exists. The quality of all profiles is zero, because in the quality function of the FRM only applications should be considered. The goal of the FRM is to maximize the quality of applications, not of the system services. System services are indirectly optimized by deactivating them and releasing their acquired resources, thus allowing the FRM to activate a profile of an application with higher quality.

In contrast, if the FRM activates a profile of an application which needs a system service and the system service is actually deactivated, the FRM automatically activates a profile of the system service in which the service is activated. This profile change is initiated by the FRM as the application requests the resource associated to the primitive of the system service. This reconfiguration is automatically carried out as in the profile in which the service is deactivated the service itself would block the use of the primitive by holding the associated resource. Thus, a profile of an application which uses a system service and a profile of this service in which the service is deactivated is never activated by the FRM as this would mean activating an infeasible profile configuration. This would be detected by the FRM as the sum of all minimal resource requirements of the resource associated with the primitive would exceed the available amount of this resource.

From the point of the FRM no special mechanism is required for this as the FRM treads the system service as a normal application task. All the reconfiguration is done in the enter/leave methods between the profiles of the system service.

To simplify the example only the requirements for FPGA resource and for bandwidth are shown in the table, additional resource requirements like memory or CPU are hidden. The minimum and maximum required area on the FPGA is constant in the software and hardware only profile. Once activated these profiles do not allocate additional area on the FPGA. Both profiles hold the required area on the FPGA handed over by the reconfiguration profile. This is the reason why the maximal assignment delay is zero between these profiles as no new circuit has to be loaded on the FPGA when the profiles are activated. As the reconfiguration of the FPGA takes time (in this example up to 10 ms) the minimum dwell time for the reconfiguration profile is 10 ms. After this time the system is reconfigured to the other configuration and the FRM can force the Ethernet in the target profile. The acceptance test for over-allocated states ensures that this multiple profile reconfiguration does not violate any time constraints.

The resource 'bandwidth' has a special significance for this communication system service: it is the resource which the service provides to the system. In the terminology of TEReCS this resource is a system primitive. The maximum bandwidth provided is 100 MBit/s, which can only be provided by the hardware profile of the Ethernet switch. The hardware/software variant can only provide 14 MBit/s. Therefore, the Ethernet switch blocks in the software profile the unavailable bandwidth by allocating 86 MBit/s. This guarantees that the FRM does not activate this variant if a bandwidth larger than 14 Mbit/s is required. This kind of modeling is necessary because the FRM operates on a fixed quantity of resources. The use case in which the software switch of the switch is activated can be called *partially used* (less than 14 MBit/s are required by the applications) and the use case for the hardware switch to be activated can be called *partially used* (more than 14 MBit/s are required). This shows that the identification of the use case – which implementation to activate – directly depends on the currently required primitive / resource bandwidth by other applications or system services.

Optimization example

To show the benefit of the self-optimizing RCOS/RTOS the following example scenario is used. The scenario consists of three components, which define profiles: the presented Ethernet switch component, a bandwidth manager, and a self-optimizing application. In Table 8.1$_{102}$ the defined settings of the profiles, which the components defined, are shown.

Bandwidth manager The Ethernet switch is responsible for delivering packets to components on the node and for transit traffic through the node. To guarantee communication under hard real-time conditions bandwidth reservation is applied. By means of the bandwidth manager applications from other nodes can reserve bandwidth in the Ethernet component of this node. The manager allocates the amount of bandwidth at the local FRM for the remote application.

The Bandwidth manager defines only one profile because it can neither be deactivated nor has any implementation alternatives. It is implemented in software, thus no FPGA resources are required. The minimum and maximum bandwidth requirements range from 1 MBit/s to 100 Mbit/s with an assignment delay of 15 ms. This delay allows the activation of the Ethernet switch's software implementation in order to release FPGA resources. If more bandwidth is required enough time is available to load the hardware implementation. 1 MBit/s is reserved for the communication between the bandwidth managers of the whole communication system (e.g. for the reservation protocol). The remaining bandwidth is allocated if reservations are made by the bandwidth manager.

Self-optimizing application The self-optimizing application is a component that tries to optimize another application component (e.g., a mechatronic feedback controller). The optimization process can be accelerated, e.g., by a floating point unit (FPU) implemented in the FPGA. The PowerPC processor of our system does not provide an integrated FPU, so if no FPU is loaded into the FPGA, floating point calculations are performed in software with a large overhead. The FPU requires 3000 slices of the FPGA resource and accelerates a 32-bit floating point multiplication by the factor of 44. For system services and application 7.000 slices of the FPGA are available in the system. This means, only the hardware Ethernet switch or the FPU can be executed on the FPGA, but not both at the same time. The FRM deactivates the hardware Ethernet switch by activating the software profile of the switch if a bandwidth less than 14 MBit/s is required in the system. If a higher bandwidth is required, the floating point acceleration of the application is deactivated and the hardware switch is activated.

8.5. Chapter Conclusion

In this chapter the extension of an offline OS configurator to the online case was discussed. The combination of modeling the OS reconfiguration options and the management concerning different resource profiles of the applications were presented. By the integration of TEReCS and the FRM into a RTOS a self-optimizing real-time operating system (SO-RTOS) is derived. Such an OS adapts itself with the help of the FRM to the needs of the current applications executed on top of it. Using this technique services can be deactivated and resource freed can be put at the applications' disposal. The real-time capability of the FRM ensures that only such services are deactivated, which can be reactivated under hard-real time constrains, if required by application tasks.

9. Application Design Flow

The design process of mechatronic systems today is based on high-level design tools like MATLAB/SIMULINK [1] or CAMeL-VIEW [2], that support modeling, analysis, and synthesis of a feedback controller. Due to complexity designing mechatronic systems is a challenging task. A good approach to minimize programming errors is to ease the design process by these high-level tools. To enable engineers to easily use the FRM and respectively the profile model, they must be integrated into a high-level design process.

In this chapter a method is presented, which allows semi-automatic code generation for mechatronic components by specifying additional information. This enables a process to become a resource-aware agent by using the FRM. These components describe their reconfiguration by means of hybrid statecharts, the design technique developed for self-optimzing systems in the CRC614 (3.1_{15}). The technique of automatic creation of profiles is introduced on the basis of the first version of the shuttle's active suspension system (comp. Section $3.8.1_{23}$). The design has to ensure safety even in case of dynamic resource allocation.

The design approach of self-optimizing systems, as briefly introduced in Section $3.8.1_{24}$, is extended to support the design of resource-aware agents. In Section 9.1 the model (the hybrid statechart) is equipped with additional semantic information to derive the profiles automatically.

9.1. Extended Modeling

The extension of the modeling is presented by means of the first version of the SURF demonstrator (comp. Section $3.8.1_{23}$).

Resource Requirements

For each specific control state of a hybrid statechart the required resources are determined by simply accumulating its own resource requirements, as well as the state specific resource requirements of all

---
[1] http://www.mathworks.com/products/family_overview.html
[2] ixtronics.de/English/CAMeLView.htm

9. Application Design Flow

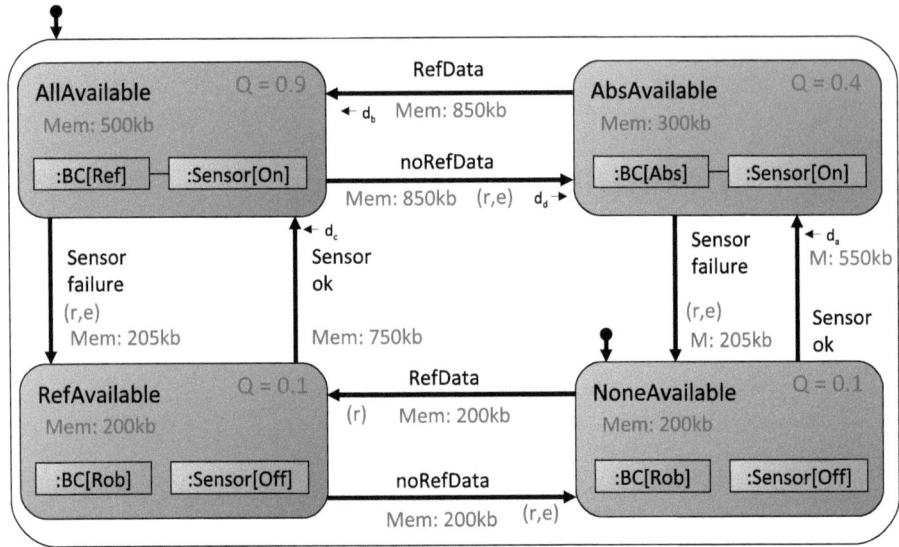

Figure 9.1.: State Chart Example with extensions.

sub-components of the configuration in this state. As the employed approach already supports automatic code generation, the model contains the required knowledge about the resource requirements. In Figure 9.1$_{108}$ the memory requirements are visualized below the state names. If a transition leads to the exchange of controllers, they require resources as well. In case of fading between control algorithms, the required amount is the sum of the source and the target states plus additional resources for the fading itself (here 50 kb). Atomic transitions just require the resources of the target state plus some for the state vector (here 5 kb). As the transitions between the state NoneAvailable and the state RefAvailable do not lead to reconfiguration, they require just as much memory, as the source and the target states (200 kb). Besides some relevant attributes, which can be derived automatically from the standard design model, some more specific semantic information has to be added.

Quality

At first, in order to support rating of a profile's quality a quality to each state of the statechart has to be assigned. It is visualized in a state's upper right corner. Both states NoneAvailable and RefAvailable, have the lowest quality, because they apply the same controller.

Transition Flags

In order to derive the profiles automatically, a transition obtains capabilities. A transition might be:

- *required*,
- *blockable* due to resource constraints,
- or can be *enforced* to change resource consumption.

As a profile should not prohibit transitions that are indispensable for the safety of the system, these transitions are marked as *required* (r) (e.g. the sensor.failure-transitions in Figure 9.1_{108}). Transitions, which can be safely blocked to restrict the future allocation of resources, are named *blockable*. As all transitions that are not required are blockable, only the required ones are marked. In the example of the SURF module, the transitions to AllAvailable are blockable, because they are just increasing the comfort and are not required to guarantee safety.

When the FRM demands resources and therefore initiates a profile-switch, the monitor of the SURF module needs to reside in a state in which it is still functioning. For example, it can not switch into a mode where required inputs are not available (eg. due to a communication failure). To achieve this, the FRM distinguishes between enforceable and non-enforceable transitions. Therefore, in addition to the marks *blockable/required*, a transition is marked as *enforceable (e)/non-enforceable*. An enforceable transition fires either when it is triggered by an event and a true guard – as usual transitions, *or* when it is triggered by the FRM. As *enforceable* and *non-enforceable* are mutually exclusive only *enforceable* transitions are marked. Looking at the example: the transitions *from* AllAvailable are enforceable, because all input signals that are required in the target states are available in AllAvailable, too. In contrast to that switching *to* AllAvailable may only occur, when the according inputs are available and not due to resource requirements. Note that the distinction between *blockable/required*, as well as the mark *enforceable/non-enforceable* has to be taken into account, when formal verification of the system is considered. This is required due to the fact that restricting the application in the usable states during run-time is cutting down the functionality of the application. The formal verification has to check whether the required functionality is still assured in the restricted statecharts.

9.2. Profile Synthesis

These resource requirements, the state's profile qualities, and the outlined classification of the transitions as required/blockable, or enforceable/non-enforceable are used further to automatically derive profiles for an agent.

9. Application Design Flow

The idea is: simply to relate each profile to a subset of the discrete states of the statechart. The synthesis algorithm generates profiles by assigning multiple values to the maximum quantity of the different profiles. After that the algorithm assigns states to these profiles using the following rules:

- In each profile only such states are included, which require equal or less resources than the maximum quantity specified in the profile. Thus, each profile blocks transitions, which result in entering a state that requires more resources than the maximum quantity for that profile.
- Required transitions cannot be blocked by the FRM and therefore a profile has to be closed with respect to all states that are reachable via required transitions.
- The FRM can additionally switch between profiles by enforcing specific transitions.

In the following the approach is described in a formal way.

Formalization

Let $G = (N, T)$ denote to the statechart of the application related graph with nodes N, representing the states of the statechart, and $T \subseteq N \times N$, its transitions. Additionally the subsets T_r, T_b, and T_e of required, blockable, and enforceable transitions with $T = T_r \cup T_b$ and $T_r \cap T_b = \emptyset$ are distinguished. Any subgraph (N', T') with $N' \subseteq N$ and $T' \subseteq T \cap (N' \times N')$ could be a possible profile.

The quality of each state $n \in N$ is denoted by $q : N \to I\!R$. For a group of states $N' \subseteq N$ this value is assigned using the definition $q(N') := \max\{q(n) | n \in N'\}$. The obtainable quality of a profile is given by the maximum of all contained state's qualities ($q((N,T)) = q(N)$).

The required amount for all m resources, of each state and transition, is accordingly assigned by the function $r : (N \cup T) \to I\!R^m$ and can be interpreted as the cost of the subgraph. For simplicity, without the loss of generality, the amount of each resource is mapped to $I\!R$ in this formalization. For a subgraph (N', T') the element-wise cost maxima is used as costs ($r((N',T')) := \max(\{(r_1,\ldots,r_m) | \forall i \in [1:m] \, \exists x \in N' \cup T' : r(x) = (x_1, \ldots, x_i, \ldots, x_m) \wedge x_i = r_i\})$. For any $r, s \in I\!R^m$ $r \leq s$, iff for all $i \in [1:m]$ holds $r_i \leq s_i$ and $r < s$ iff $r \leq s$ and there exists $i \in [1:m]$ with $r_i < s_i$.

Optimal Permanent Profiles

The FRM usually expects that an agent is able to stay permanently within the assigned profile. For such permanent profiles of an agent, it is required that the related subgraph is closed with respect to required transitions.

Definition 1. *A profile (N', T') is permanent, iff for all required edges $(n', n) \in T_r \cap N' \times N$ holds $n \in N'$.*

9.2. Profile Synthesis

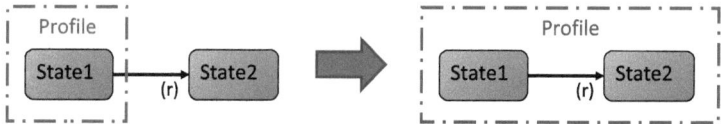

Figure 9.2.: Permanent profile.

Figure 9.2$_{111}$ demonstrates the definition of permanent profiles.

Further with $[(N', T')]$ is denoted the largest subgraph of (N', T'), which is closed with respect to required transitions. It can be computed as the largest fix-point of the function C on profiles defined as $C((N', T')) := (N'', T'')$ with $N'' = \{n \in N' | \forall (n, n') \in T_r : n' \in N'\}$ and $T'' = T' \cap (N'' \times N'')$. The set of permanent profiles is further closed under union and intersection.

The number of profiles can be exponential in the number of states (which might itself be rather large). Thus, it is not of interest to compute all possible profiles but only "optimal" ones.

Informally, a profile is optimal when no other profile contains it, which offers a higher or equal quality for the same or less costs. Optimality is formalized in the following definition:

Definition 2. *A permanent profile* (N', T') *is optimal, iff no other permanent profile* (N'', T'') *exists with:*

$$(N', T') \subset (N'', T'') \tag{9.1}$$
$$r((N', T')) \geq r((N'', T'')) \tag{9.2}$$
$$q((N', T')) \leq q((N'', T'')) \tag{9.3}$$

The three conditions above describe that no larger profile (9.1) with equal or less costs (9.2) exists, which has the same or higher quality (9.3). As the quality is implied by set containment, Condition 9.3 can simply be skipped. Also Condition 9.2 can be made more strict, as a larger set of nodes and transitions by definition can only be as cheap as the contained one, but not cheaper. Thus:

$$(N', T') \subset (N'', T'') \tag{9.4}$$
$$r((N', T')) = r((N'', T'')). \tag{9.5}$$

If such a profile (N'', T'') exists, this fact is called: (N'', T'') *dominates* (N', T'). The full graph (N, T) is by definition an optimal one as Condition 9.4 cannot be fulfilled by any other profile. Figure 9.3$_{112}$ illustrates the definition of optimal profiles. As state one and state two have the same cost (200kb memory), state one alone is not an optimal profile. Thus, the optimal profile in this figure contains state one and state two, because state two can be implemented without additionally memory.

9. Application Design Flow

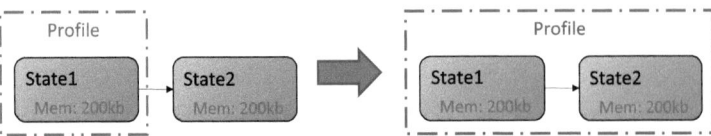

Figure 9.3.: Optimal profile.

To compute optimal profiles efficiently, the following idea is used:

Lemma 4. *For a given optimal profile* (N', T') *with costs* $k = r((N', T'))$ *for any* $k' \leq k$, *an optimal profile* $(N_{k'}, T_{k'})$ *with maximal* $r((N_{k'}, T_{k'})) \leq k'$ *can be constructed as follows:*

- $N'' = N' - \{n \in N' | r(n) > k'\}$,
- $T'' = T' - \{t \in T' | r(t) > k'\}$, *and*
- $(N_{k'}, T_{k'}) = [(N'', T'')]$.

Proof. The proof is done by contradiction: assuming $(N_{k'}, T_{k'})$ is constructed as outlined above and is not the optimal profile. Thus, there exists a profile (N''', T''') which dominates $(N_{k'}, T_{k'})$. This means that (N''', T''') fulfills the Conditions 9.4_{111} and 9.5_{111} w.r.t. the profile $(N_{k'}, T_{k'})$: $(N''', T''') \supset (N_{k'}, T_{k'})$ and $k'' = r((N''', T''')) = k'$. It must hold $(N''', T''') \subseteq (N', T')$, because otherwise $(N''', T''') \cup (N', T')$ dominates (N', T') and, thus, (N', T') would not be optimal.

Thus, it must exist an element $x \in (N''' \cup T''') - (N_{k'} \cup T_{k'})$, otherwise the assumed profile would not dominate $(N_{k'}, T_{k'})$. For $x \in (N' \cup T') - (N'' \cup T'')$ it can be concluded that $r(x) > k'$ and, thus, $r((N''', T''')) > k'$ which contradicts the assumption. Thus, finally none such profile (N''', T''') which dominates $(N_{k'}, T_{k'})$ can exist and thus the profile $(N_{k'}, T_{k'})$ is an optimal one.

As no $(N''', T''') \supset (N_{k'}, T_{k'})$ can exist, $k''' = r((N_{k'}, T_{k'}))$ is always maximal with respect to the upper bound k'. ∎

Therefore, the optimal profile can be computed for a given $k' \in I\!R^m$ by simply starting with the full graph and applying the outlined steps.

Besides optimality of permanent profiles, the enforceable transition between two profiles is required to allow the framework to enforce a switch between these two profiles.

Using the set of enforceable transitions T_e, it can formally be defined whether the framework can enforce the transition from one profile to another.

Definition 3. *A profile* (N', T') *is reachable from a profile* (N'', T'') *iff for all* $n \in N'' - N'$ *there exists* $(n, n') \in T_e$ *with* $n' \in N'$. *The short notation is:* $(N'', T'') \rightarrow_e (N', T')$.

9.2. Profile Synthesis

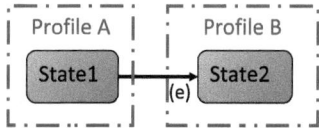

Figure 9.4.: Reachable profile.

Figure 9.4[113] depicts this definition.

For the relation between optimal profiles and reachability, the following Lemma 5[113] can be proven, which ensures that each time a non optimal profile is reachable, also the larger optimal profile is reachable. Thus, the attention can be restricted to optional profiles when reachability is considered.

Lemma 5. *For profiles* (N', T'), (N'', T''), *and* (N''', T''') *with* $(N', T') \subseteq (N'', T'')$ *it holds*

$$(N''', T''') \rightarrow_e (N', T') \Rightarrow (N''', T''') \rightarrow_e (N'', T'')$$

Proof. Follows directly from Definition 3[112], as $N''' - N' \supseteq N''' - N''$. ∎

Temporary Profiles

An optimal profile may not be reachable from another one due to the fact that not enough enforceable transitions in T_e exist. Then *temporary* profiles are added to the profile graph to improve the connectivity using a series of steps and to accept non optimal profiles temporarily.

As mentioned before not every subgraph (N', T') can be used as a profile because the subgraph must be permanent, thus closed with respect to required transitions T_r. To compute a profile of a subgraph which is permanent, the core of a subgraph is defined as follows:

Definition 4. (N'', T'') *is the* core *of the subgraph* (N', T') *iff for all edges* $(n, n') \in T_r \cap (N'' \times N)$ *holds* $n' \in N'$

Thus, the core of a subgraph (N', T') contains no node, that has a required edge (T_r) pointing to a node which is not in N'. The example of Figure 9.5[114] illustrates the definition of a core.

$N'' = \{n \in N' | \forall (n, n') \in T_r : n' \in N'\}$ and $T'' = T \cap (N'' \times N'')$ can be computed to construct the largest core (N''', T''') of (N', T') with respect to T_r. As short notation $[(N', T')]^{CORE}$ is used for this maximal core.

The problem to realize a transition between two optimal profiles relates to the question of finding a series of temporary profiles (*attractor*) with respect to the enforceable transitions T_e.

9. Application Design Flow

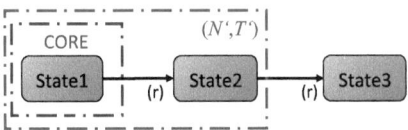

Figure 9.5.: A core of a subgraph

Definition 5. *A sequence of profiles* $\{(N_i, T_i) | i \in I\!N\}$ *is an* attractor *for the profile* (N'', T'') *with respect to the enforceable transition set* T_e *and the required transition set* T_r *iff forall* $n \in N_{i+1}$ *and* $(n, n') \in T_r$ *exists* $(n', n'') \in T_e$ *with* $n'' \in N_i$ *and* $(N_0, T_0) = (N'', T'')$.

An attractor has to be constructed for the target profile (N'', T'') in such a way that a path backwards to our start profile (N', T') exists.

The *attractor* is computed, starting with the target profile. By looking for additional states of the current profile where any possible, required step can be continued in such a manner that the current profile is reached, the next profile is computed. If the extension leads to a profile which includes the source profile, a sequence of temporary profiles is found, otherwise no indirect connection can be established.

For the set of required steps T_r and the enforceable transitions T_e, the *attractor* of (N'', T'') can be computed as follows:

1. Initially set $N_0 = N''$ and $T_0 = T''$.

2. Compute $N'_{i+1} = N_i \cup \{n \in N - N_i | \exists (n, n') \in T_e \land n' \in N_i\}$ and $T'_{i+1} = T \cap (N'_{i+1} \times N'_{i+1})$ from (N_i, T_i).

3. Compute the core $(N''_{i+1}, T''_{i+1}) = [(N'_{i+1}, T'_{i+1})]^{CORE}$ of (N'_{i+1}, T'_{i+1}) and determine the next profile (N_{i+1}, T_{i+1}) by $N_{i+1} = N''_{i+1} \cup N_i$ and $T_{i+1} = T \cap (N_{i+1} \times N_{i+1})$.

4. Repeat with step 2 until the start profile (N', T') is included $((N_{i+1}, T_{i+1}) \supseteq (N', T'))$ or the expansion has terminated $((N_{i+1}, T_{i+1}) = (N_i, T_i))$.

By construction, it holds that $(N_{i+1}, T_{i+1}) \supseteq (N_i, T_i)$. Because of this, the profiles of the attractor $\{(N_i, T_i) | i \in I\!N\}$ are monotonously increasing but not necessarily strictly.

If no $(N_i, T_i) \supseteq (N', T')$ has been found, there is in fact no possible sequence of temporary profiles leading from (N', T') to (N'', T''). Otherwise, if a profile (N_p, T_p), which contains (N', T'), has been found such a sequence is constructed using the computed profiles of the attractor in opposite ordering

$$(N', T') \supseteq (N_p, T_p) \to_{r,e} \cdots \to_{r,e} (N_0, T_0) = (N'', T'').$$

9.2. Profile Synthesis

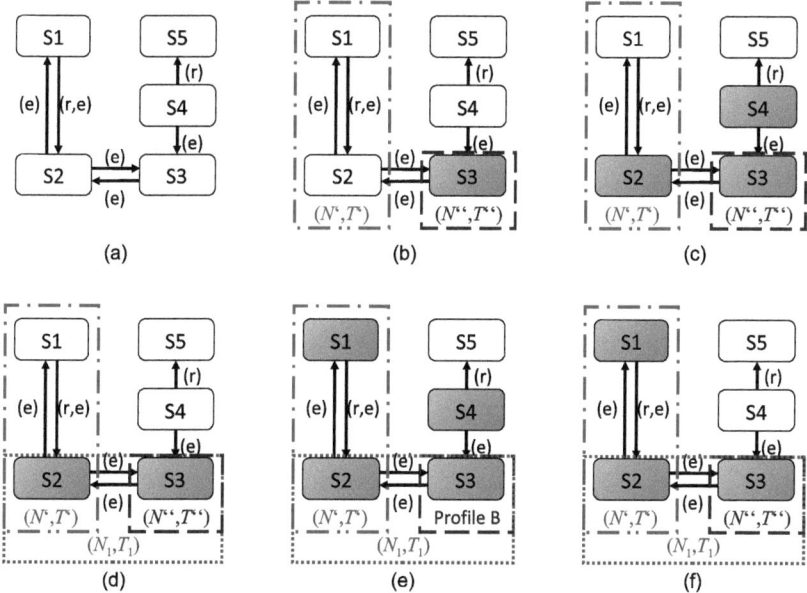

Figure 9.6.: Example of attractor computation.

Figure 9.6₁₁₅ shows an example how an attractor is computed with the previously described steps. In 9.6₁₁₅(a) an example statechart is introduced. 9.6₁₁₅(b) shows two optimal profiles: profile (N', T') (state 1 and 2) and profile (N'', T'') (state 3). An attractor is now constructed to get a sequence of enforceable profiles from profile (N', T') to profile (N'', T''). Also step 1 of the algorithm is illustrated in 9.6₁₁₅(a). The step initializes $N_0 = N''$ and $T_0 = T''$. This is represented by the marked state, in this case only state 3. In 9.6₁₁₅(c) step 2 is applied, thus N_1' and T_1' are computed. N_1' is the union of N_0 (state 3) and the states which have enforceable edges to N_0 (state 2 and 4). Step 3 is applied in 9.6₁₁₅(d), thus the largest core of (N_1', T_1') is computed, which is state 2, and the next profile (N_1, T_1) is computed by uniting N_0 and $[(N_1', T_1')]^{CORE}$, which contains the states 2 and 3. By using only the core and the profile (N_0, T_0) state 4 is eliminated which was an element of the intermediate subgraph N_1' of the previous step. State 4 is eliminated because it has a required edge to state 5 which is not included in the profile (N_0, T_0). As profile (N_1, T_1) does not include profile (N', T') (state 1 is missing) the next iteration of the computation is started and step 2 is applied again. In 9.6₁₁₅(e) N_2' and T_2' are computed. Again N_2' is the union of N_1 (state 2 and 3) and the states which

9. Application Design Flow

have required transitions to nodes of N_1 (state 1 and 4). Step 3 is applied in 9.6_{115}(f), thus the next profile is computed using the core of (N_2', T_2'). The next profile (N_2, T_2) contains the states 1, 2 and 3. As (N', T') is a subset of (N_2, T_2) an attractor is found and the computation is finished.

Using the procedure outlined above, the connections in the profile graph can be constructed as follows. A direct edge is added, if for two optimal profiles of the graph (N', T') and (N'', T'') it holds $(N', T') \rightarrow_e (N'', T'')$. Otherwise, the procedure outlined above is used to derive additionally required temporary profiles. Finally, if all possible profile connections have been established, the graph can be optimized further by keeping between two optimal profiles only the shortest one, using the Floyd-Warshall all shortest path algorithm.

Compute Profile Graphs

To generate profiles with different resource requirements the m dimensional space of resources is partitioned using an equidistant set K of upper resource limits which is derived as follows:

1. determine for each dimension the minima and maxima ($\min_i = \min(\{r_i(x)|x \in N \cup T\})$ and $\max_i = \max(\{r_i(x)|x \in N \cup T\})$),
2. determine a number of steps $s_i \geq 1$ for each dimension, and
3. chose K as $K_1 \times \cdots \times K_m$ with $K_i = \{c|\exists j \in [0:s_i] : c = \min_i + (\max_i - \min_i)/s_i * j\}$.

The set K is then used to generate optimal profiles according to the elements of K. To advance the reachability between the optimal profiles, it is attempted to generate temporary profiles between optimal profiles which are not directly reachable from each other.

An upper bound for the complexity of the profile computation can be estimated as follows: every application of the algorithm, which is sketched in Lemma 4_{112} to generate optimal profiles for a given resource boundary, will cost at most $|N| + |T|$ steps. The algorithm is applied for every resource boundary of the set K, thus $|K|$ times. Thus, computing all optimal profiles is then in $O(|K| * (|N| + |T|))$. For each optimal profile it has to be checked whether another optimal profile is directly reachable, thus for every state of a optimal profile it has to be checked whether an enforceable transition exists to a state of another optimal profile. This computation of the maximal $|K|$ profiles with at most $2 * (|K|)^2$ direct transitions is in $O(|K|^2 * (|N| + |T|))$. For the indirect connections via temporary profiles $O((|N| + |T|)^2)$ is required for computing the attractors and, thus, the algorithm to compute them is in $O(|K|^2 * (|N| + |T|)^2)$. Optimizing the profile graph using the Floyd-Warshall all shortest path algorithm for $|K|$ profiles (nodes) is in $O(|K|^3)$. Thus, the overall algorithmic effort is $O(|K|^2 * (|N| + |T|)^2 + |K|^3)$.

The maximal required duration (WCET) of the transitions between the different profiles is derived from the transition's deadline information of the hybrid statechart.

If the transition itself does not require more resources than the source state, the transition deadline determines the allocation delay for resources which are configurable in background. If the transition itself requires more resources than the source state, then the delay is the time that the agent can wait before the transition execution has to start.

9.3. Case Study

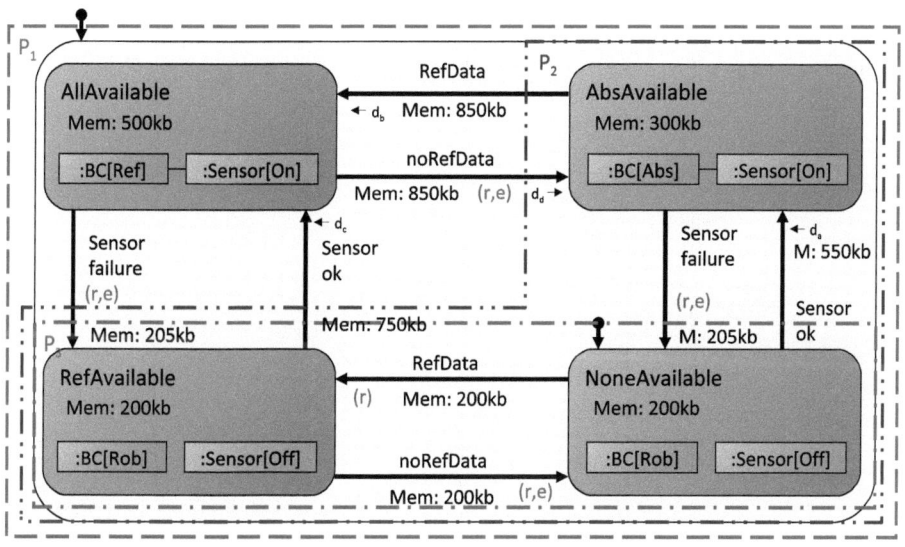

Figure 9.7.: State Chart Example with extensions and profiles.

As an example, the presented algorithm is used to derive profiles from the extended model of the first version of the SURF demonstrator. Three different profiles are obtained (cf. Figure 9.7): ρ_3 consisting of the states RefAvailable and NoneAvailable, ρ_2 consisting of additionally AbsAvailable and ρ_1 consisting of all states. The three profiles differ in their quality and resource usage.

9.4. Chapter Conclusion

In this chapter a technique to ease the creation of profiles at low costs is presented. Base statecharts of the applications are extended to semi-automatically generate different profiles. This helps to minimize the effort which has to be spent during the design phase, when using the flexible resource framework. Additionally required steps can be seamlessly integrated into the standard process for the design of mechatronic systems. The presented results can also be employed for other embedded system classes, if alternative operation modes with distinct resource requirements are present that can but not necessarily have to be used. So this technique is applicable not only to self-optimizing systems.

Part IV.

RTOS for Self-optimizing Mechatronic Systems - Evaluation

10. Case Studies

This chapter focuses on application examples. Thus, only an application specific sight how the FRM can be used is presented. Especially it is shown how applications can be modeled to use the profile framework. Interaction between applications through the FRM is afterwards shown in the successive Chapter 11. First two demonstrators of the CRC 614 (Section 10.1: active suspension system and Section 10.2$_{123}$: self-optimizing drive) are modeled into profiles. It is shown how these applications can make use of additional resources and/or can provide unused resources to other applications' disposal. A special mechanism, which is comparable to the acute stress response of the human body and amplifies the FRM approach, is presented in Section 10.3$_{124}$. This mechanism enables the flexible release of resources for the handling of emergencies in self-optimizing mechatronic systems. The case study in Subsection 10.3.1$_{126}$, the operation point assignment, illustrates the benefit of this mechanism.

10.1. Active Suspension System

As described in Section 3.8.1$_{23}$ the active suspension system comes with four operation modes: passive, relative, absolute and reference. The different operation modes need not only different power ratings like supply pressure but also different resources on the information processing level, like memory and computation time.

The described complex control strategies are extensions of the simple ones. Hence, the required amount of resources increases depending on the chosen mode of operation. Additional sensors have to be evaluated as well as more calculations have to be done on the basis of the new sensor data and when the reference mode is active the storage component requires more memory to store the track data. The calculation of the actuating variables has to fulfil hard real-time conditions and must be performed within every time step depending on the sampling rate. On the other hand the processing of the accessed track information can be done anytime, if it is only finished before the vehicle arrives at the respective track section.

As at run-time the operation modes are changed, different resources are required over time. Thus, an application of the flexible resource management tenders for this control structure. First, profiles can be defined that require different amounts of resources, but which also differ in their quality of control.

10. Case Studies

Actually, the basic relative control is sufficient to travel across a track without any risks. Thus, a minimum amount of resources is required for this operation mode. However, the comfort suffers from this strategy on rough tracks. Activating the skyhook control and the disturbance compensation requires the maximum amount of resources but also maximizes the comfort. For medium comfort with a medium amount of required resources the disturbance compensation can be turned off keeping the skyhook control activated.

The self-optimizing control of the active suspension system enables the activation and deactivation of the additional control strategies depending on the actual situation. Due to optimization inside the OCM, reconfiguration between the control strategies can be triggered by the cognitive operator, by the reflective operator due to sensor failure or (from a higher control strategy to a lower) by the FRM due to profile changes. The active suspension system can specify the most likely mode of operation for future track sections. Hence, the amount of resources can be made available to the FRM for planning. In case of deviation from the expected track characteristics a change to an operation mode that requires more resources may be anyhow reasonable. The FRM either ensures that the resources are available to the active suspension system in time or forces the active suspension system to a profile with lower requirements because other subsystems need the resources more urgently. In this way the resources of the entire system can be used efficiently retaining a high degree of performance of the subsystems.

Hence, the following apportionment into profiles is reasonable:

Profile 1 This profile includes all modes of operations. The application, thus the cognitive respectively the reflective operator, decides in this profile, which mode is activated. Hence, the actual resource requirements are changing over time, not used resources can be put temporarily at other applications' disposal. The defined quality in this profile is the highest, because the self-optimizing process of the OCM can select the actually best control strategy. As mentioned before depending on the current environmental conditions even the best quality can be reached without the skyhook and disturbance compensation.

Profile 2 This profile only includes the passive, relative and absolute mode. The complex control strategy with disturbance compensation is not included. The maximal resource requirements are therefore lower than in the first profile. Of course the quality of control is lower on rough tracks. Thus, the defined quality in this profile is also lower.

Profile 3 This profile only includes the passive mode and is not meant for normal operation. The profile can be unlocked by the reflective operator in case of an emergency of another component to free additionally resources for failure recovery. This profile can be used in combination with the active stress response method for mechatronic systems described in Section 10.3_{124}.

Thus, the FRM can put unused resources of the active suspension module temporarily at other applications' disposal on tracks with few disturbances dynamically.

In Section 9.3_{117} the active suspension system was also used as a case study for the semi-automatic generation of profiles. In that section the algorithm generates an additional profile because in the example a finer resolution for the resource memory was chosen. The additional profile only uses the relative mode. It is to mention that the passive mode is not modeled in the statechart model.

10.2. Self-optimizing Drive Control

The drive control (comp. Section $3.8.2_{28}$) was designed especially for the use of the FRM. The OCM of the drive control has different operation modes with different resource consumptions. A special mode of this application is, that on one side it wants to get directives according the aspired resource consumptions from the FRM and on the other side wants to select the operation mode in special cases by itself and thus override resource constrains. Because of that, multiple profiles are defined, which include the same operation modes and thus the same minimal and maximal resource consumption. The differences between the profiles are that they strive for different average resource consumption and a different quality. With the average resource requirements the FRM tells the application, which amount of resources it should maximally strive for. Furthermore the application can allocate resources up to the maximally specified value of its actually activated profile, thus all operation modes can be activated at any time in each profile. The OCM adjusts the quality of the profiles based on the quality of control at run-time, which can be reached with the average resource requirements of the respective profile. Through the changing qualities of the profiles and the profile changes through the FRM the FRM is integrated into the system of objectives (comp. Section 3.3_{17}) of the drive control OCM. The change of profile is an external objective for the OCM, this change specifies the average resource requirements, which the OCM tries to keep. The change of the quality is a feedback towards the FRM. If the OCM decides to use an operation mode with less resource requirements than the maximum resource requirements, the unused resources can be to other applications' disposal in the typical FRM manner until the self-optimizing drive control needs them. The FRM guarantees a rearrangement of resources on time, thus no hart real-time constrains are violated.

An additional aspect of the self-optimizing drive control is the implementation of control algorithms in software (C++) and hardware (VHDL). With this a certain quality of control can be selectively realized with different types of resources. In the software implementation the algorithm requires CPU time, in the hardware implementation space on the FPGA. These two variations can be mapped to different profiles with the same quality. The FRM activates the variation which aids to improve the overall system quality. For example, if the quality of another application can be improved through an accelerator in hardware on the FPGA, the FRM can choose the profile of the software variant of the self-optimizing drive control and free space on the FPGA for the hardware accelerator.

10.3. Acute Stress Response in Resource Management

Self-optimizing techniques can be used to react on hazards or detected failures. A problem is that most of these techniques require additional resources to handle the hazard and compensate the failure. To deal with this fact a modeling technique is to keep these additional resources as backup in every profile of the application using the FRM model. If these resources are unused they could be put to other applications' disposal. The disadvantage of this approach is on the one hand that the maximum number of existing system resources must be as high as the sum of all worst case requirements in order to fulfill these requests even when all applications request their resources at once. On the other hand, there could be non-critical applications, e.g. some comfort modules, which could be deactivated or executed in a very limited mode in case of a failure of another component and free additional resources. Thus, these applications could unlock special profiles, which are not allowed to be executed in regular mode of operation.

To overcome this limitation and better handle unanticipated faults, a generic self-organizing scheme was developed to enable self-optimizing mechatronic systems to exploit the ability of their parts to adapt the resource requirements. The scheme is inspired by the *acute stress response* of a living being. It enables in the case of an emergency that all available resources are assigned in such a manner that the threat can be addressed with priority. The advantage of this approach is that not the FRM decides if an application switches to a profile with lower resource requirements but the applications itself can decide how to react.

A constraint for resource assignment in case of a hazard or detected failure is that the assignment should be as fast as possible, to start advanced self-optimizing countermeasures. Thus, for this case the "normal" optimization process inside the FRM could take too long.

Acute Stress Response of living beings

The American physiologist Walter Cannon published the "Fight-or-flight"-theory in 1929, also known as *acute stress response* [Can29]. It describes the reaction of humans and animals to threats. In such "stress" situations specific physiological actions are taking place by the sympathetic nervous system of the organism as an automatic regulation system without the intervention of conscious thought. The hormone epinephrine is released, which causes the organism to release energy to react on the threat (fight or flight). For example, digestion is slowed down to consume less energy.

Acute Stress Response for self-optimizing applications

The acute stress response behavior can be imitated inside the OCMs with support of the FRM. The main idea is, when an OCM of the system detects a threat for the system, the agent releases virtual epinephrine. Every OCM can then decide how to react on the distributed epinephrine. Non-critical OCMs can unlock profiles with lower resource consumptions to free resources and thus permit the OCM, which released the epinephrine, to handle the threat more appropriately by switching in a profile of an emergency category with higher resource consumptions to handle the threat.

Concrete the epinephrine carries the information how much additional resources the OCM, which released the epinephrine, requires activating its optimal profile to handle the threat. Like the blood system in an organism, the FRM distributes the epinephrine to the other OCMs. The epinephrine is injected to the OCMs and they can react on the epinephrine by unlocking special profiles with lower resource requirements. If an OCM is only responsible for comfort it could for example switch to an *"Off"* profile with no or minimal resource requirements. A resource conflict could not arise by activating this profile, as this special profile of the application has lower resource requirements than the current configuration of the application. Thus, only schedulability of the profile reconfiguration has to be checked. The derived scheduling criteria of Theorem 3_{74} in Chapter 6_{63} is reused for this purpose. The OCM "consumes" the epinephrine, this means the information inside the epinephrine how much resources are still required is updated. Then the resource manager distributes the updated epinephrine to the next OCM. Even if no resources are required anymore, every OCM has information about the threat and can react accordingly. This procedure has the advantage that a faster self-organized reallocation of the resources is achieved, than in the case of the regular resource optimization of the FRM.

The normal operation of other hard real-time applications must continue, even in a case of a hazard. Thus, the distribution of the epinephrine must be integrated into the real-time scheduling, without violating deadlines of other hard real-time applications. To ensure this, the reaction of the OCMs to the epinephrine (consuming it) is specified to be done in a short, constant time (a WCET has to be declared). This makes the integration into the schedule easier. Due to task switching costs an immediate distribution of the epinephrine to all applications can lead to problems. Thus, a trade-off between fast distribution and the overhead of the distribution is chosen: the distribution is done in two different modes. The applications are assigned to these different modes according to the activation time of their next instance. Tasks with a short activation time (e.g. tasks with a short period) get the epinephrine with the next regular task execution. Thus, the tasks have to implement in their profile main function the query whether epinephrine is released and if so react on the epinephrine. As stated before, this reaction must be done in a short constant period of time. This time is integrated in the calculation of the normal WCET of the main function. Applications with a higher activation time get

10. Case Studies

the epinephrine in the idle time, if the idle time is long enough for the distribution. To increase the idle time, soft-real time tasks can specify if they can be left out in case of hazards.

As reaction is required fast, the system does not search for an optimal solution. Activation of tasks with lower resource requirements than the current requirements can be done without checking resource dependencies. To avoid resource conflicts for the activation of emergency profiles with higher resource requirements it only has to be checked if enough resources are freed by other applications. Thus, the resources specified in the epinephrine have been consumed. Profile reconfiguration can then be done under the same conditions as reconfiguration due to over-allocation (comp. Section 6.1_{63}), depending on the current and to activate state of the profile configurations.

This approach has the disadvantage that the resources are not freed immediately and it could happen that the required resources are never freed at all. This is the case, when the hazard also affects other applications, which also release epinephrine, e.g. when half of the mechatronic system is destroyed. On the other side the approach assures the correct execution of other applications as a classical system does. Thus, the methodology allots that basic safety countermeasures of the applications to react to threats are always included in a every profile. So the basic countermeasures can be initiated without any delay, as no additional resources are required. More advanced responses, which require additional resources can only be employed if the required additional resources are made available due to the stress response.

10.3.1. Operating Point Assignment and the Acute Stress Response

The CRC614 demonstrator of the operating point assignment (comp. Section $3.8.2_{28}$) is used as a case study to show how the acute stress response can be used by self-optimizing applications.

In this case study the OCM is modeled as four different profiles *"Self-Optimizing max"*, *"Self-Optimizing min"*, *"Fail-Operation min"* and *"Fail-Operation max"*. The self-optimizing profiles are for normal mode of operation, including simple fail-operational behavior. The fail-operation profiles are only for fail-operation mode in case of a failure. The *"Fail-Operation max"* profile includes advanced self-optimizing techniques to handle the failure. All states belonging to one profile build the state space that can be reached when the profile is active. In Figure 10.1_{127} the inclusion of the states in profiles is depicted by assigning the related profile numbers. The required resources of the controller are always the same if the system is in operation. Therefore, the *Control* state must be contained in all profiles. The resource requirements of the reflective operator in contrast vary depending on the current profile. In the *"Self-Optimizing min/max"* profiles all three parallel states are active while in *"Fail-Operation min/max"* they are subsequently disabled. The cognitive operator can be switched off if required. Therefore, the states *Pre-Adjust*, *Optimizing*, and *Decision Making*, which require high calculation-resources, are only supported in the *"Self-Optimizing max"* profile.

10.3. Acute Stress Response in Resource Management

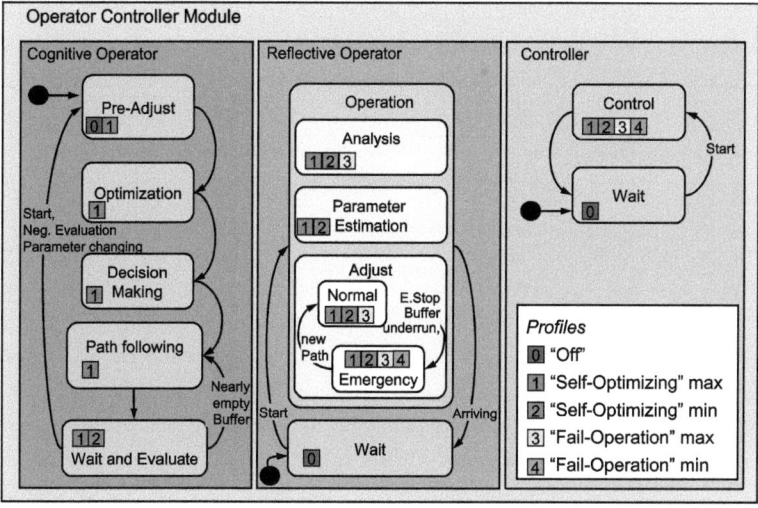

Figure 10.1.: States and profiles of the *Operating Point Assignment* OCM.

On the other hand, the *Path Following* and *Wait and Evaluate* states, which need just less resources, are also in the *"Self-Optimizing min"* profile. None of this states are present in any of the *"Fail-Operation min/max"* profiles. This reflects the fact that the decoupling of the OCM concept permits to suspend the complete cognitive operator at any time. A recovering of the cognitive features will lead to a possible restart of the optimization cycle.

As pointed out earlier this OCM can use the acute stress response, provided by the FRM. The OCM can utilize both directions supported by the acute stress response: first, it can free resources in normal mode of operation if some other application releases virtual epinephrine. This is done by making the *"Self-Optimizing min"* profile available for activation through the acute stress response in the FRM. Second, if the OCM itself is in the normal *Analysis* state, a substate of the reflective operator, and detects a problem, normally it will release virtual epinephrine through the acute stress response in the FRM to get additional resources for countermeasures within the *Emergency* substate of the *Analysis* state. The *Analysis* state therefore is not included in the *"Fail-Operation min"* profile.

10. Case Studies

The *"Fail-Operation max"* profile, which contains the *Emergency* substate of the *Analysis* state, is activated if the acute stress response can gather enough resources to activate it. In the meantime the current profile can be executed (as basic emergency management is included in every profile, which does not require additional resources), the *"Fail-Operation min"* profile is unlocked (because fast reactions are required and the cognitive operator is switched off automatically), and the acute stress response tries to free resources. These basic countermeasures are not as efficient as the optimized countermeasures supported together with the *Analysis* in the *"Fail-Operation max"*, but sufficient in the sense of dependability.

With this special case study a generic concept for the OCMs and its self-coordination via the RTOS have been presented. The concept emulate the acute stress response of natural beings in the case of an emergency such that available resources are reallocated to address a given threat. The outlined self-coordinated adaptation of the system enhances the dependability of systems as resources are employed more focused. It is also helpful for unanticipated problems as the investment of more resources to the control of misbehaving mechatronic subsystems is in many cases sufficient to compensate smaller systematic failures. This approach allows a more flexible self-optimizing reaction on failures.

10.4. Chapter Conclusion

In this chapter several case studies how the FRM concept can be used in applications and system services have been presented. It was shown that in the self-optimizing scenario applications can easily utilize the FRM approach, due to their dynamic resource allocation during run-time. The OCM concept, its modular structure and the feature of multiple configurations make it easy for the different self-optimizing modules to provide different profiles and thus to be enabled to consume additional resources for self-optimization. In an example scenario the freed resources are utilized by a self-optimizing application. In the last case study the concept of acute stress response in resource management of self-optimizing applications was presented. This concept allows a more flexible reaction in emergency situations and enables a new level of self-optimization.

11. Simulation

The focus of the previous chapter was to demonstrate how applications and system services can be modeled in profiles to utilize the FRM approach. This chapter presents an evaluation of the FRM approach concentrating on the interaction between the applications through the FRM. Beside the implementation of the FRM for the operating system DREAMS, the FRM concept was implemented on top of the TrueTime library for simulation purpose. TrueTime is a simulator for networked and embedded control systems and is based on MATLAB/Simulink. In focus of this thesis is the evaluation of the FRM approach by means of this simulator. In Section 11.1 TrueTime and the FRM simulator on top of TrueTime are introduced.

The simulator is used to evaluate two categories. First, concrete application examples are used and executed on one processor (Section 11.2_{132}). Second, the FRM approach is evaluated through randomly generated applications to test the approach with a high number of applications (Section 11.3_{140}).

11.1. The TrueTime and MATLAB/Simulink Based Simulator

TrueTime [OHC07, CHL$^+$03] facilitates co-simulation of controller task execution in real-time kernels, network transmissions, and continuous plant dynamics. TrueTime simulates controllers and the operating system on the controllers. A great benefit of TrueTime is that tasks can be implemented as MATLAB/Simulink block diagrams, C++ or via M-Files (the MATLAB script language). Even mixed implementations can be carried out on top of TrueTime, for example C++ files which call MATLAB/Simulink block diagrams. This feature allows to integrate MATLAB/Simulink block diagrams into tasks, which use the FRM.

TrueTime splits the execution of tasks into segments and calls one segment after another according to the selected scheduler (e.g. EDF). The return value of a segment is interpreted as the execution time of the segment itself but can also be zero. A negative return value is interpreted as the last segment of the task in the case of an aperiodic task or of the task instance in case of a periodic task. Thus, the ex-

11. Simulation

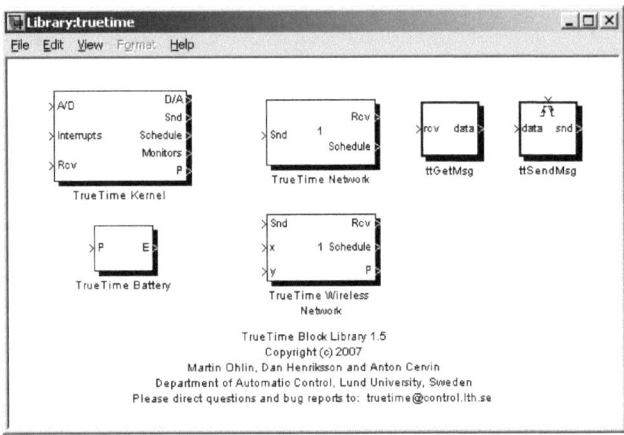

Figure 11.1.: Simulink blocks of the TrueTime library.

ecution time is not measured by TrueTime and has to be specified by the programmer of the segment. Of course, the return value can be calculated during runtime, for instance to consider loop iterations depending on input values. TrueTime executes each segment completely without preemption, even if the scheduling strategy would preempt the execution. Therefore, communication between tasks or the environment (I/O to plant or other controllers/tasks) has to be placed into different segments to get correct semantic behavior of the simulation. TrueTime has a rich API which provides the most common operating system primitives for task management (incl. scheduling), communication, I/O, synchronization and interrupt handling.

As TrueTime is integrated into MATLAB/Simulink it is easy to access MATLAB functionality like plotting different variables over time. The center of the TrueTime environment is the TrueTime kernel. The TrueTime kernel is a MATLAB/Simulink block (comp. Figure 11.1), which simulates the microcontroller incl. the operating system. The important inputs of this block are: a vector of analog input values (eg. for connecting sensors to the controller), an interrupt line and a port to receive messages (which can be connected to TrueTime network blocks). In the context of this thesis interesting outputs of the TrueTime kernel block are: a vector of analog output values (eg. for connecting actuators to the controller), a port to send messages to a TrueTime network block, and a schedule vector, which maps each task into one of its three schedule states. The three states of a task can be: finished, waiting for CPU assignment (ready) or running. This schedule can be easily plotted with MATLAB. The example in Figure 11.2_{131} shows a screenshot of a schedule vector with

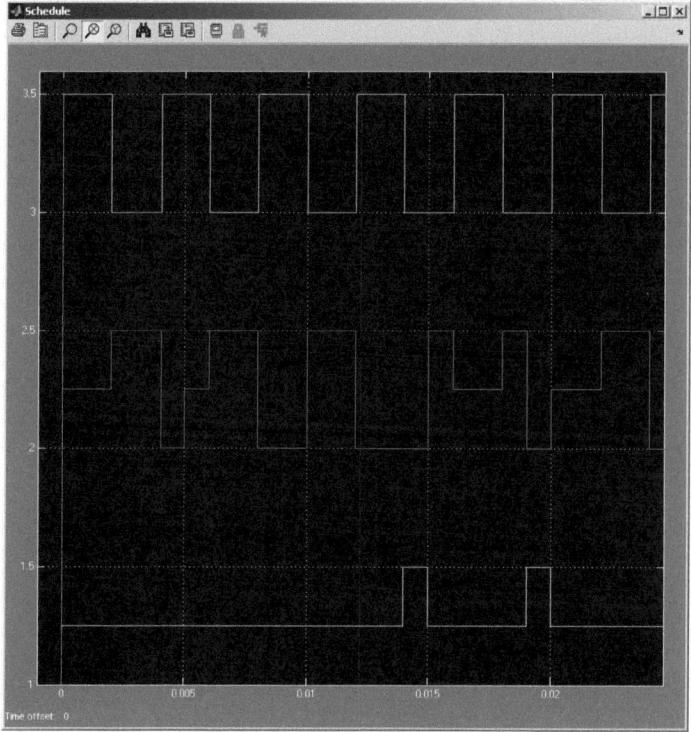

Figure 11.2.: Example plot of a TrueTime schedule vector.

three applications. In the figure the three states of the second application are mapped to the following values: $finished = 2$, $ready = 2.25$ and $running = 2.5$.

FRM on TrueTime

Some of the CRC 614 demonstrators are executed on DSPACE hardware, which includes a proprietary operating system. Thus, no FRM support is available. As mechatronic systems are often modeled and simulated with MATLAB/Simulink and the same is true for self-optimizing mechatronic systems, especially for the control part, most demonstrators of the CRC614 are modeled in MATLAB/Simulink (including controller and plant). Thus, an early integration in the FRM environment is possible with

11. Simulation

the FRM simulator based on MATLAB/Simulink. The goal is to simulate a timely correct behavior of the OCMs using the FRM. Thus, the behavior of profile switches on the controller can be tested.

The TrueTime version of the FRM uses the same codebase as the version for DREAMS. Therewith the FRM is executed within an abstraction layer. The abstraction layer maps the DREAMS operating system API to the TrueTime API. This eases the portability of the FRM to the TrueTime platform. Because of the different execution characteristic of TrueTime a complete transparent use of TrueTime instead of DREAMS is not feasible. On the one hand, the main function of the tasks of each profile and the FRM optimization must be split into different segments, depending on their communication behavior with the environment. On the other hand, some TrueTime specific API calls have to be integrated into the FRM code.

The FRM is built on top of TrueTime by means of three different threads: An optimization thread, a thread for configurations due to optimization and a thread for configuration due to exhaustion. The main reason for modeling the configurations as different threads is to visualize the different configurations in MATLAB/Simulink. With this approach it is easier to distinguish between the different types of configurations when looking on the schedule plot. The optimization thread is executed with the lowest priority of all tasks and because EDF is used as scheduling strategy the deadline is set to infinity. This models the behavior of executing the optimizations in the idle time of the processor, when no other task is ready for execution. The optimization process is also mapped on segments to simulate the preemption.

Figure 11.3_{133} shows an example schedule plot. The plot shows two applications, the idle task, the optimization task and the reconfigurations (due to optimization and due to exhaustion). As the optimization is executed instead of the idle task the idle task is never executed.

11.2. Evaluation Using Case Studies

To show the benefit of using the FRM in a system, applications are executed virtually on one node. In this following scenario the applications share resources of one node through the FRM approach. The OCMs of the application and the plants are executed on the TrueTime/MATLAB/Simulink based simulation platform of the FRM. On top of the simulator the following applications are simulated as a simulation case study.

Three applications are used in this example: A controller for an inverse pendulum, a servo motor and a cognitive operator. The applications are executed on one simulation node, thus competing for the resources of the node. The resources of the node are:

- 10 FPGA slots,

11.2. Evaluation Using Case Studies

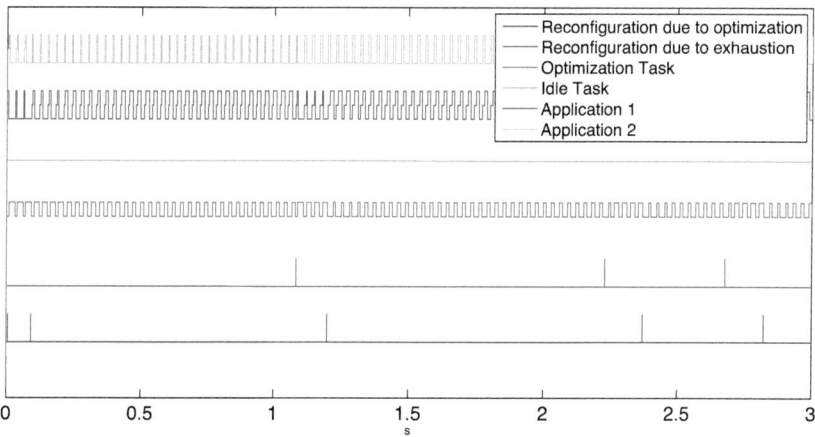

Figure 11.3.: A schedule plot in the FRM simulator.

- 100% CPU utilization.

For simplicity the resource memory is not shown, as in this example the resource memory has no impact. In the following the three applications are described and their profiles are introduced.

Inverse Pendulum

The inverse pendulum is a simple example application inside the CRC 614 to demonstrate the power of FPGA based control, the exchange of the control algorithm through run-time reconfiguration of the FPGA as well as the migration of the control algorithm from the FPGA to a software implementation. The goal is to swing up the bob of a pendulum and after that hold the bob standing up. For this the pendulum is fixed at a horizontal rail which can be moved by an electrical motor which is controlled by the controller of this application.

The inverse pendulum is an example for an application which is *only* a providing task. It has only one profile with changing resource requirements. Not used resources can be put at other applications' disposal. The used model supports only the swing up implemented in the FPGA. After the pendulum stands up, the control strategy is changed to hold the pendulum. This mode starts execution on the FPGA but is than migrated to the software implementation, which only uses a small area on the FPGA for I/O. The pendulum can fall down e.g. due to external forces. In this case the control strategy to

11. Simulation

Profile name	Profile quality	Resource requirements				min. dwell time
		CPU utilization		FPGA in Slices		
		min	max	min	max	
Profile 1	0.5	0.01	0.3	1	6	-

Table 11.1.: The profile of the inverse pendulum.

swing up the pendulum in the FPGA is activated again until the pendulum stands up again. Table 11.1$_{134}$ shows the parameters of the defined profile.

Servo Motor

This application is a simple controller which operates a servo motor. The controller can be executed with different sampling rates. It is important to mention that, both modes are sufficient to control the servo motor but have a different quality of control. Two different sampling rates are mapped into two different profiles:

Profile 1 Here, the controller is executed with a low frequency.

Profile 2 Here, the controller is executed with a high frequency. Thus, this profile has a higher quality value, because the quality of control is increased.

The servo motor is thus an application which can consume additional CPU resource by activating its second profile. Table 11.2 shows the parameters of the two profiles.

Profile name	Profile quality	Resource requirements				min. dwell time
		CPU utilization		FPGA in Slices		
		min	max	min	max	
Profile 1	0.2	0.08	0.08	0	0	-
Profile 2	0.5	0.33	0.33	0	0	-

Table 11.2.: The profile of the servo motor.

Cognitive Operator

This application is a cognitive operator of a fictive OCM. The cognitive operator tries to optimize continuously its controller and is modeled in two profiles:

11.2. Evaluation Using Case Studies

Profile 1 This is a pure software variant of the cognitive operator.

Profile 2 This is a variant of the cognitive operator with is accelerated by an FPGA based circuit. This could be for example a matrix multiplication. The quality is higher than in profile 1 as the optimization is more accurate.

Table 11.3 shows the parameters of the defined profiles.

Profile name	Profile quality	Resource requirements				min. dwell time
		CPU utilization		FPGA in Slices		
		min	max	min	max	
Profile 1	0.1	0.6	0.6	0	0	-
Profile 2	0.5	0.6	0.6	7	7	-

Table 11.3.: The profile of the cognitive operator.

11.2.1. Interaction Between the Applications

At system start, the FRM activates the first profile of each application, as this is the defined start configuration. It has passed the check for a guarantee configuration.

The inverse pendulum, as the providing task, is the *driving force* in this example. Depending on what resources are currently only reserved for but not allocated by the inverse pendulum the FRM activates the profile with the higher quality of the cognitive operator respectively servo motor controller.

In the example scenario the pendulum starts with the bob fallen down. Thus, the controller, executed in the FPGA profile, starts to swing up the bob. Figure 11.4_{136} shows the mode of the controller (swing up or hold) in one graph and the output of the FPGA module of the controller in the other graph. The output is the value set to the actuator – the electrical motor. Around time 6.8s the bob stands up and the controller switches the mode from swing up to hold. After a short stabilizing phase (~6.8s to ~9.3s) the bob stands up and only small corrections have to be made by the controller to hold the bob up (time ~9.3s and higher).

Around time 14.74s the controller switches from the FPGA implementation to the software implementation. The second graph in Figure 11.4_{136} shows only the output of the FPGA controller. Thus, the output of this module is zero after the software implementation is activated. The FPGA implementation is disabled and 5 FPGA slices are released until the swing up mode is required again. This is the case if – e.g. through external irritation – the bob falls down. Summarized the controller

11. Simulation

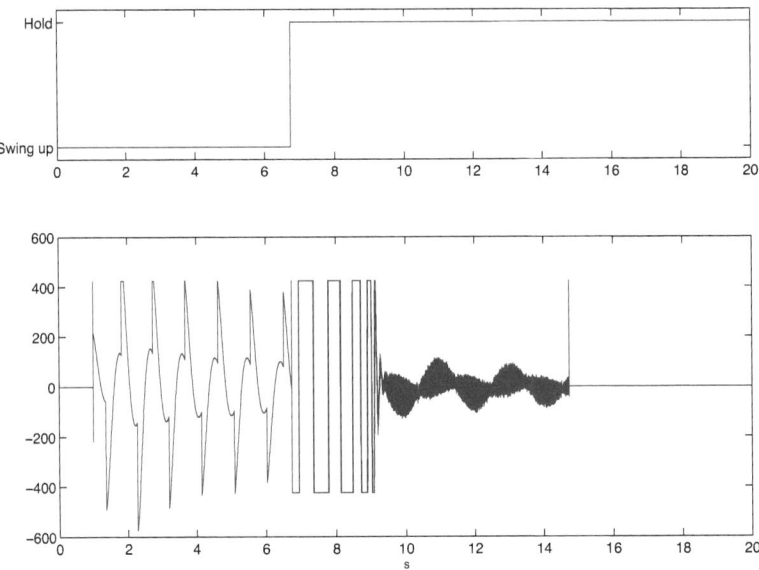

Figure 11.4.: Control State and FPGA controller output of the pendulum.

of the pendulum requires until ~14.74s 1% CPU utilization and 6 FPGA slices in the FPGA implementation. After ~14.74s the controller requires 30% CPU utilization and only 1 FPGA slice in the software implementation. Before ~14.74s the not used CPU utilization from the pendulum controller can be put at other applications' disposal. After ~14.74s the unused FPGA slices can be put at other applications' disposal.

Figure 11.5_{137} shows the profile assignment for time segment 0ms to 25ms. At system start all applications are executed in their first profile. The optimization algorithm of the FRM starts to search for a better configuration in the system's idle time. In this example, after ~9ms the FRM finds and activates a better configuration, where the unused CPU utilization from the pendulum is put to the servo motor controller's disposal, by activating the second profile of the servo motor controller.

The cognitive operator can not be executed in its second profile as not enough FPGA slices are currently available to activate the profile parallel with the FPGA implementation of the pendulum. The second profile of the servo motor controller has a higher quality than the first one, thus the overall quality of the system is improved by switching this controller's profile. The activated configuration is

11.2. Evaluation Using Case Studies

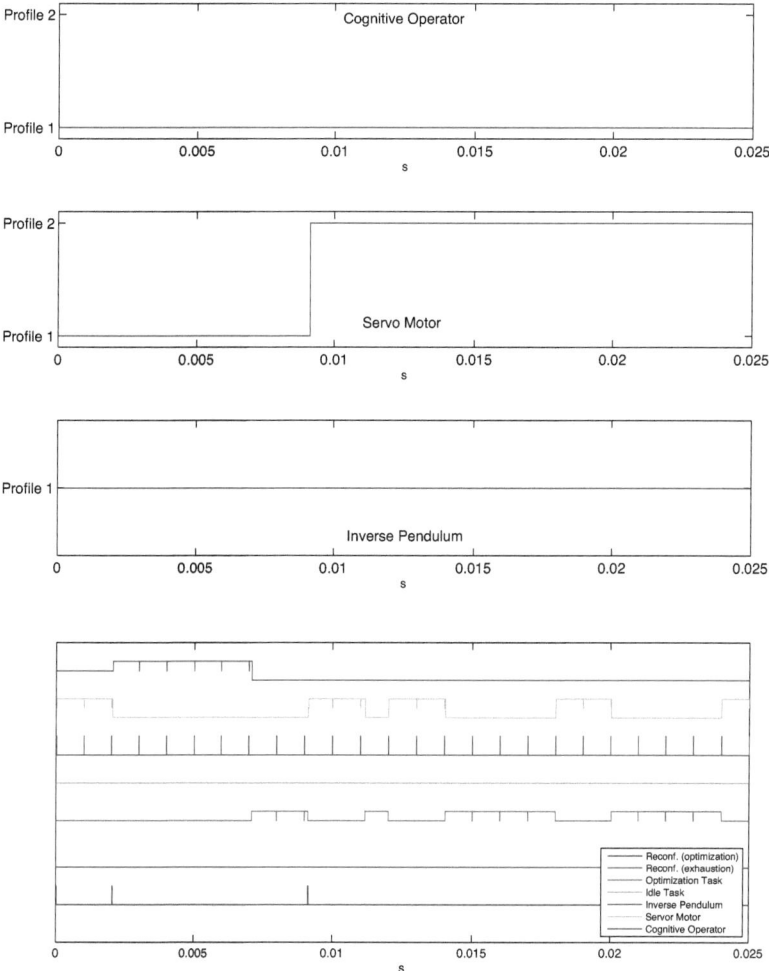

Figure 11.5.: Profiles and schedule plot 0s to 0.025s.

an over-allocated configuration, as the specified maximum amount of the resource CPU of the active profiles exceed 100%. For the case of a conflict – the pendulum allocates CPU utilization – the FRM has arranged the plan to reconfigure the servo motor controller back to the first profile, thus activate

11. Simulation

the start configuration. In this example, this is the only guaranteed configuration.

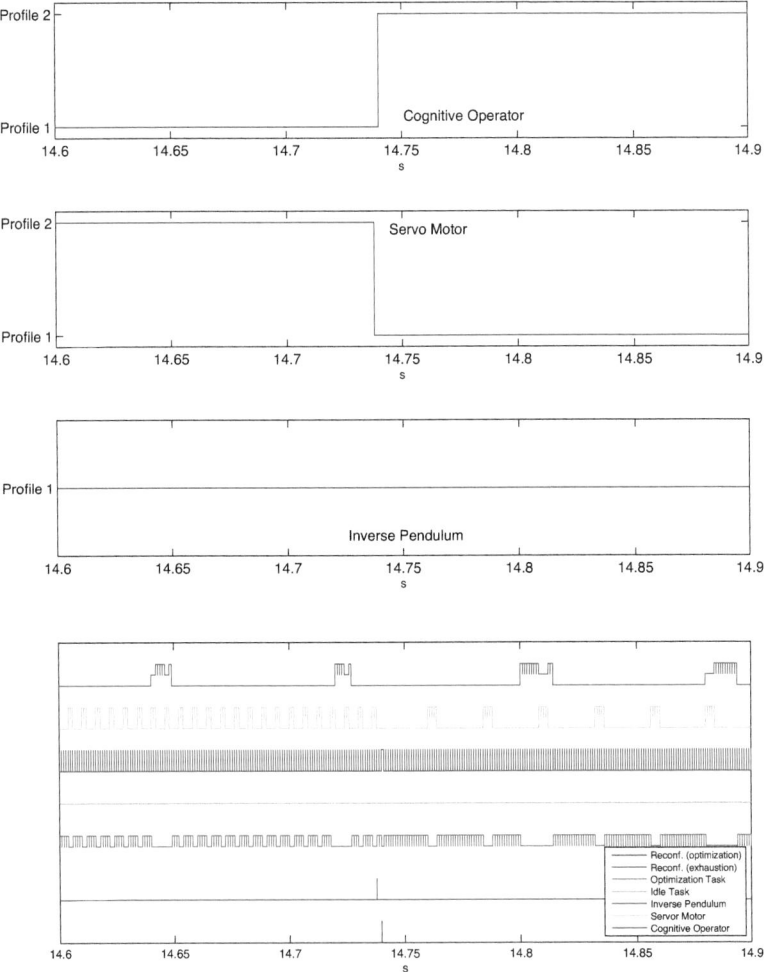

Figure 11.6.: Profiles and schedule plot 14.6s to 14.9s.

11.2. Evaluation Using Case Studies

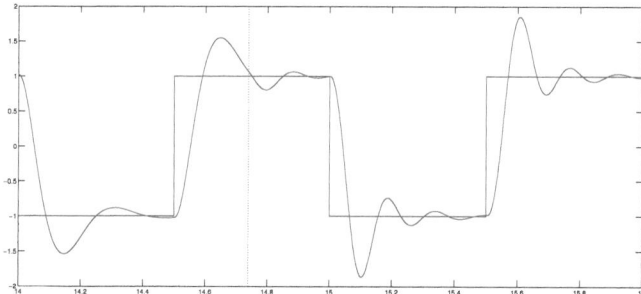

Figure 11.7.: The reference and feedback value for the sensor motor controller.

The activated profile configuration is the best possible configuration, for the case the pendulum is executed in the FPGA implementation. Thus, this configuration is kept activated until the pendulum switches to the software implementation at time ~14.74s (comp. 11.6) and arises a resource conflict. The conflict results from the allocation of the CPU utilization by the pendulum, which is put at the sensor motor controller's disposal. The FRM than executes the way back plan and forces the servo motor to the first profile. The schedule plot in Figure 11.6 shows the changing frequency in the execution of servo motor controller, thus the change utilization at the time of profile change. Additionally the graph shows that the computation of the optimization task and the servo motor controller is more often interrupted as the inverse pendulum requires more CPU utilization in the software implementation. Figure 11.7 shows the reference value for the controller and the simulated output of the sensor connected to servo motor model. The dashed vertical line at ~14.74s illustrates the time when the profile with the better sample rate (higher CPU utilization) is switched to the profile with the lower sample rate (lower CPU utilization) due to this conflict. The different quality of control between the different profiles can be seen in the overshoots. The height of the overshoots around 14.15s and 14.65s is lower, where the profile with the quality profile is executed, than the height overshoots around 15.1s and 15.6s, where the profile with the lower quality is executed.

Shortly after solving the conflict the FRM finds another configuration with a higher quality, which could be activated under the current resource consumptions. In the better configuration the cognitive operator is switched to its second profile, where it consumes the FPGA resources temporarily not used by the pendulum in the software implementation. Thus, the quality of the cognitive operator is improved by accelerating its optimization with an FPGA based coprocessor (e.g. for matrix operation).

With this example it can be seen that the FRM puts the unused resources of the pendulum at other applications' disposal as intended. The quality of the servo motor and the cognitive operator has been improved with the temporary unused resources.

11.3. Evaluation Using Randomized Simulation

To test the FRM concept with a huge number of applications, an application simulator was developed. These simulations allow to generate a broad diversity of test cases. The applications are generated randomly within specified boundaries. Per application, three profiles are generated, with the quality of 0.1, 0.3 and 0.5. Transitions exist from the first profile to the second profile and vice versa as well as from the second profile to the third profile and vice versa. The min/max values per resource are generated randomly but growing from the first profile to the second profile and from the second to the third profile. Additionally, multiple probability distributions for the allocation behavior inside each profile can be specified. The applications have no real internal functionality besides simulating the specified allocation behavior. The simulator can run in batch mode to execute several application scenarios and different FRM optimization algorithms / improvements consecutively.

To make the simulations of different optimization algorithms and improvements of the FRM approach comparable, the pseudo random generator is started with the same random seed. Thus, the different versions of the FRM face the same application resource requests. For the simple greedy heuristic, the parameter for the depth of the breadth first search, after the FRM activates the best found configuration it has found so fare, is varied over time. The complete method is used as a reference because it calculates the optimum for the resource assignment by using global knowledge. The complete algorithm uses the same criteria to decide if a better over-allocated configuration should be activated according to current resource consumption and the probabilistic information about future resource requirements. In the simulation, the complete algorithm returns to the TrueTime based simulator zero as calculation time for finding a better profile configuration. Thus, in the simulation, the complete algorithm knows immediately the best configuration to activate. Due to the memory consumption, as described in Section 7.2, and the computation time the complete algorithm is not applicable during run-time. The algorithm therefore only delivers the upper bound for an optimization algorithm.

The execution of all applications in their initial profiles can be seen as a lower bound. The initial configuration is a guaranteed configuration. This would be equivalent to the case the FRM approach would not be used and the applications do not share resources by over-allocation.

In Figure 11.8_{141}, the outcomes of different simulation runs are presented. On the one hand sim-

11.3. Evaluation Using Randomized Simulation

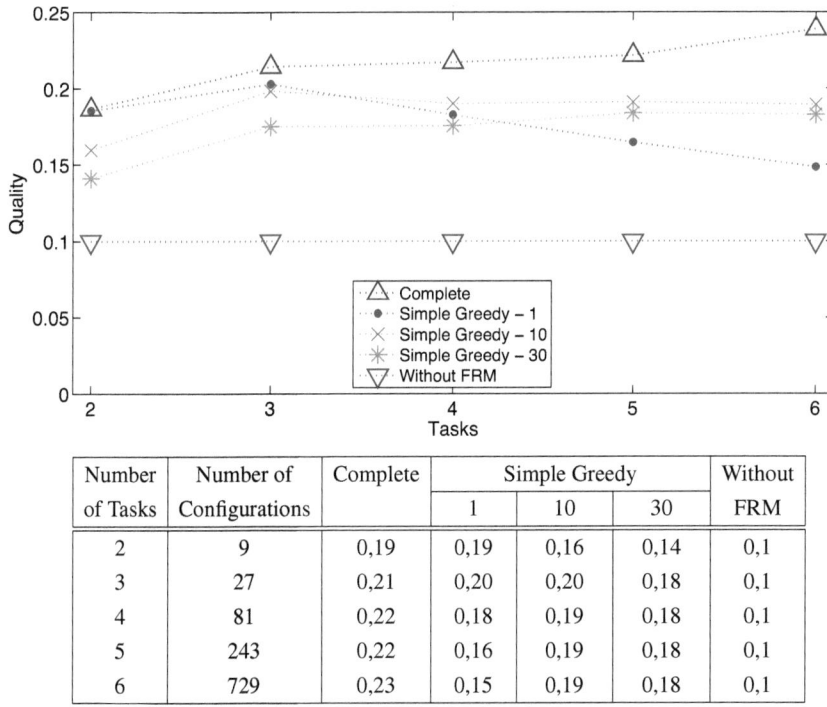

Number	Number of	Complete	Simple Greedy			Without
of Tasks	Configurations		1	10	30	FRM
2	9	0,19	0,19	0,16	0,14	0,1
3	27	0,21	0,20	0,20	0,18	0,1
4	81	0,22	0,18	0,19	0,18	0,1
5	243	0,22	0,16	0,19	0,18	0,1
6	729	0,23	0,15	0,19	0,18	0,1

Figure 11.8.: Simulation results.

ulation is executed with a different number of applications, on the other hand different optimization algorithms are used: the complete algorithm and the simple greedy algorithm. The simple greedy is executed with different depths of the breadth first search: 1, 10 and 30. Every plotted point is the mean value of ten simulation runs with different randomly generated application sets. The different versions of the algorithm are all executed with the same inputs (application sets and allocation behavior). The comparison ends at six applications per run as the simulation time for the complete algorithm would have taken too long due to the exponential growth.

It can be seen that the simple greedy algorithm performs very well for a simulation range up to six applications per node. As expected, the simple greedy is losing quality with the exponential growth of configurations that have to be checked when the number of applications is increased. When using

11. Simulation

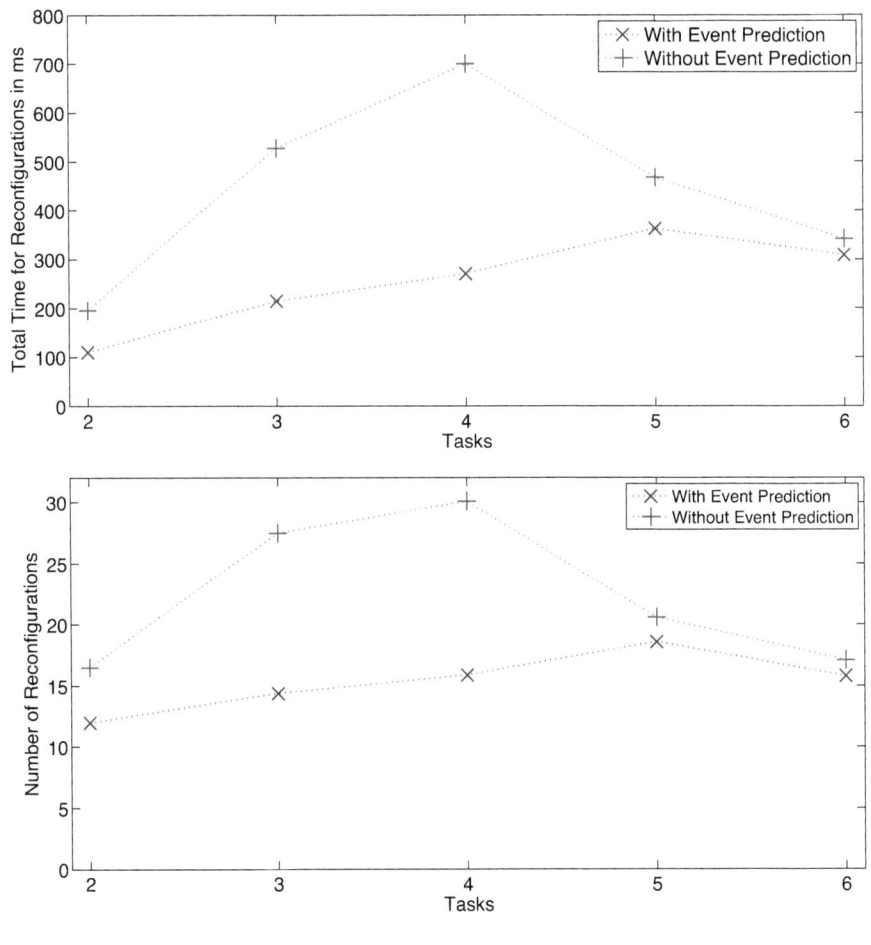

Figure 11.9.: Comparison: FRM with and without event prediction.

six applications with three profiles each, the number of configurations is $3^6 = 729$.

The quality of the simple greedy algorithm depends on the different values for the depth of the breadth first search and the number of applications. Simple greedy-1 means that the algorithm, as soon as it finds a better configuration, uses it as a candidate for activation. Simple greedy-30 means that the algorithm checks 30 configurations consecutively and takes the best configuration as a candidate for activation. For small number of applications, the simple greedy-1 achieves a better result as the time for finding a better configuration is shorter as for the simple greedy-30. Thus, the simple greedy-1 activates earlier a configuration with higher quality. On the other hand, when the number of possible configurations grows, with the increased number of applications, the simple greedy-30 has a better quality. This is due to the fact that the simple greedy-1 needs more intermediate configurations to reach a configuration with a higher quality than the simple greedy-30. As this intermediate configurations are configurations due to optimization, the FRM schedules them not immediately but rather when they fit into the current schedule. Thus, it is a trade of between early activation and reconfiguration overhead. Simple greedy-10 is therefore a good compromise.

Figure 11.9_{142} shows the impact of using the even prediction. The presented results are taken from the simulation of the simple greedy-10 algorithm with event prediction enabled and disabled. The difference between the algorithms is the decision when an over-allocated configuration is used as the next candidate to activate. When the event prediction is enabled, an over-allocated configuration with a higher quality is only activated when the probability of a conflict is not too high. When the event prediction is disabled, an over-allocated configuration with a higher quality is activated if the applications which change their profiles could allocate their specified minimum of resource requirements. Thus, a conflict could arise very soon after the over-allocated configuration is activated with a high probability. The number of reconfiguration decreases, when the number of applications is increased and the event prediction is not used, as it takes longer to search the configuration space. Thus, the two variants more often activate the same over-allocated configuration. The simulation shows, that the event prediction helps to decrease the reconfiguration overhead.

11.4. Chapter Conclusion

In this chapter the evaluation of the FRM approach is presented. The benefit of using the FRM approach was first demonstrated in a case study in which the interaction between example applications from the context of the CRC 614 on the resource level was shown. Temporary unused resources were put at other applications' disposal to increase their quality. To show the benefit of the FRM approach more general, multiple randomly generated applications were executed on top of the FRM. The in the FRM used heuristic was compared to the best possible profile activation. The heuristic performs well for a small number of applications by wasting only a few resources on the profile optimization and reconfiguration. The performance increase was shown adverse execution of the applications in their standard profiles. The standard profiles can be seen as the execution of the applications without the FRM approach. Overall this evaluation shows the increased quality of the applications by exploiting

11. Simulation

the system resources in a better way than classical resource manager would do.

Part V.

Conclusion and Outlook

12. Conclusion and Outlook

In the following, the thesis is concluded (Section 12.1) and a short outlook on the next steps of improvements in the FRM concept is presented (Section 12.1).

12.1. Conclusion

In this thesis a Flexible Resource Manager (FRM) which was developed within the scope of the Collaborative Research Center 614 of the University of Paderborn is presented. The resource manager was developed with the special demands of self-optimizing mechatronic applications; respectively more general the demands of modern dynamic real-time applications. Temporarily unused resources held back for worst case scenarios are put at other applications' disposal under hard real-time constrains. The approach is called over-allocation and makes the fundament to build an RTOS for self-optimizing applications. It allows the RTOS to adapt to the current needs of the applications and to optimize the overall resource utilization of the system.

In the introduction the aim of this thesis was summarized in eight questions. In the following the questions are checked if they can be answered with the approaches presented in this thesis:

- **How to deal with higher dynamics of the application level in the operating system level (resource management, service structure)?**

  The FRM developed in this thesis, as described in Chapter 5_{49}, is built for the special dynamics in modern real-time applications. The FRM approach allows, as described in Chapter 8_{91}, to build an Self-Optimizing RTOS (SORTOS) to adapt the RTOS service structure to the current needs of the applications by deactivating unused services. With this approach, an RTOS can provide a broadness of functionality over time without wasting resources if the functionality is temporarily not required. The following questions refine this first problem.

- **How to minimize the internal waste due to worst case resource requirements?**

  The internal waste is minimized with the over-allocation concept of the FRM approach. The over-allocation allows to put temporarily unused resources, which are reserved for worst case,

12. Conclusion and Outlook

temporarily to other applications' disposal. The schedulability, thus the real-time capability, and the freeness of deadlocks have been formally proved in Chapter 6_{63}.

- **How to get information about the dynamic requirements of applications?**

  The interface to the resource manager is the Profile Framework presented in Section $5.2.1_{52}$. Through this framework, applications inform the resource manager about their resource requirements. The event prediction mechanism in the FRM, introduced in Section 7.1_{82}, refines this information and forecasts the future requirements.

- **How to decide which system service can be activated, degraded or deactivated?**

  As mentioned, the concept of a self-optimizing RTOS was described in Chapter 8_{91}. In this concept the online capable configurator Online-TERECS maps system services into profiles according to the status of the service: activated, degraded or deactivated. The configurator also models dependencies between services into the profiles via required resources. The clue is that a service blocks resources in its deactivated profile, which it provides in its activated profile. The FRM covers the profiles of system services in the same way as application profiles, thus optimizes the resource utilization (comp. Section 7.2_{87}). With this technique the FRM indirectly re-activates, degrades or deactivates the system services.

- **How to distribute freed resources to the application tasks?**

  The Profile framework, comp. Chapter $5.2.1_{52}$, allows application to specify alternative profiles with a higher resource consumption than in normal mode of operations. As the FRM is responsible for the decision which profile to activate, it can force applications, which have appropriate profiles, to consume the freed resources.

- **How to guarantee hard real-time constrains while reconfiguring resource assignment?**

  In Chapter 6_{63}, it was shown under which criteria in hard real-time systems a reconfiguration can be executed uninterruptible and immediately without violating hard real-time constrains of other applications.

- **How to make guarantees for the QoS (Quality of Service) in dynamic systems?**

  The over-allocation principle allows to give away unused – but ensured – resources of an application and also guarantees that if the application requires the resources back an allocation is timely completed.

- **How make such a system easy to use for application programmers?**

In Chapter 9_{107} a semi automatic approach was presented, which integrates the specification of profiles into the design process for mechatronic systems. This minimizes the additional expenses in the development process to use the FRM approach by generation of profiles out of hybrid state charts. Additionally, in Section 11.1_{129} a FRM simulator, which allows the execution of MATLAB/Simulink models on top of the FRM, was presented. Both enables an integration of the FRM approach in the earlier design phases of mechatronic systems.

The appliance of the FRM approach was demonstrated in Chapter 10_{121} by using application examples of the Collaborative Research Center 614. It was shown how dynamic applications, like those out of the self-optimizing context, can be modeled as multi-mode applications using the profile framework. These different profiles can be used to reduce or increase the resource consumptions of the applications to utilize the temporary freed resources to increase the system quality, e.g through additionally optimizations. Also, the concept of acute stress response in resource management of self-optimizing applications was presented. This concept allows a more flexible reaction in emergency situation and enables a new level of self-optimization.

In Chapter 11_{129} the benefit of the FRM approach was shown by means of the example execution of different self-optimizing applications on the same node and by means of multiple randomized simulations. With this simulations it is shown that the system quality is increased by using the FRM approach. A comparison to the optimal solution shows that the optimization heuristic computes a good achievement but uses less resources for the optimization.

12.2. Outlook

In the following, two improvements of the FRM are briefly described. Both approaches are currently researched in the CRC 614 and improve the optimization algorithm respectively a better approximation of future resource requests.

12.3. Look-ahead Optimization

This algorithm is more complex than the optimization algorithm presented in this thesis. This advanced approach removes the flaws of using only a single restrictive plan for conflict resolution and only searching a better configuration for the current situation of the system. For example, in the case that the best actual configuration is found and activated, this optimization algorithm plans for other possible situations the system can be in in the near future. This approach leads to better decisions about resource assignments in the FRM model than making decisions only "on the fly" when a new

12. Conclusion and Outlook

situation arises. With this in the average the algorithm can react faster with a better configuration in a new situation.

This approach solves the resource allocation problem with the aid of game-theoretical models and methods. In this algorithm a plan is computed in advance and fast access to this plan is granted to the FRM. The developed planning algorithm is based on the look-ahead approach, which is also executed during the idle time. It efficiently uses the available probabilistic information about possible events and resource requirements of applications. Probable scenarios of the system-environment interaction are explored in order to improve the overall expected system quality. This algorithm produces a robust strategy that provides the FRM with information about reaction to possible future disturbance. Of course, this algorithm tries to find as well a "strict" plan for a reconfiguration from the desired over-allocation configuration to a guaranteed allocation configuration. Only if such a roll-back plan is found the activation of the over-allocated configuration is granted. Because the worst case - i.e. every application requires the maximum amount of resources specified in their profiles - could occur and then only a roll-back plan to a guaranteed allocation configuration can solve the resource conflict. For the acceptance test, which allows an over-allocation configuration, finding such a strict roll-back plan to a guaranteed allocation state is sufficient.

The activities of a real-time system are modeled as a game between the FRM and the nature (applications). The game is represented as a tree $T = (V, E)$ of possible scenarios as well as possible moves of the players over the time. It belongs to the class of two-person games with imperfect information. Nodes V of this tree denote positions of the underlying game and edges E move from one position to another one. Set V consists of two disjoint subsets V_{max} and V_{avg}. For a node $v \in V_i$ the class V_i determines the player i who must perform the next move. Nodes $v \in V_{avg}$ (round nodes) correspond to the system configurations, square nodes designate the nature. Edges $e \in E$ denote actions of the players. An edge $e = (v_i, v_j)$ is considered to denote an event if $v_i \in V_{avg}$ and $v_j \in V_{max}$. In the opposite case edge e denotes a reaction of the system to some event. The game tree is explored in order to determine a pure strategy $S = (V', E') \in T$ that provides the FRM with an exact plan of good actions in response to the environmental changes.

The precalculated strategy is stored in a hash table. The hash table enables to organize fast access to the strategy data and to ensure timely reconfiguration of the system. The quality of the strategy depends directly on how deep the game tree is explored. Since the dimension of the game tree grows up exponentially, the complete exploration of it would be impossible even for a finite runtime of the system. Therefore, a number of heuristics are applied in order to shrink the search scope.

In this case information about the probability of events are very useful. This information is used to perform the search selectively. Also, probabilistic information about the resource requirements of the applications is used. This information makes possible to consider over-allocated system states in the future scenarios. Thus, this improves the quality of decisions in the sense of resource utilization efficiency. Additionally, the search space, when searching a way back, can be limited with the available reconfiguration time, which can be calculated with Theorem 3_{74} of Chapter 6_{63}. If the planning algorithm exceeds the available reconfiguration for a specific plan, this plan and the branch of the tree can be abolished. The discretized resource allocation steps within one profile and the fact that many profile configurations are infeasible, helps although to shrink the number of branches in the tree.

12.4. Advanced Profiles for Flexible Ressource Management

The actual FRM approach uses only the given upper and lower resource bounds, probabilities of the resource allocation and the quality of a configuration for the decision to activate an over-allocated configuration or not. This can lead into prediction failures in reassignment and force a higher reconfiguration overhead to solve conflicts and guarantee deadlines. To reduce prediction failures in reassignments further information of the allocation behavior could be used. Thus, it remains to identify subsequent time periods $[t_i, t_{i+k}]$ in profiles – referred as phases – sufficiently large, $t_{min} \leq t_{i+k} - t_i$, usable by the FRM to reassign them temporarily to other applications' disposal more efficiently than the current approach.

12.4.1. Advanced FRM Profiling

To improve the resource use efficiency the real consumption of each profile P_i in its active period $T_i := [t_s, t_e]$ could be more precisely analyzed, described by a function $f_i : time \mapsto resource$. Since the allocation behavior is unknown in advance and the aim is to segment P_i automatically, some facts must be considered. It is possibly not sufficient to define a phase each time the allocation amount changes. The same holds if T_i/t_{min} phases are used. If a phase p_k runs in $[t_i, t_{i+k}]$ it can not violate $t_{min} \leq t_{i+k} - t_i$. The resource consumption of p_k belonging to P_i is denoted with $c_{p_k}(t) \mid t \in T_i$ where, if $t \in [t_i, t_{i+k}]$ then $c_{p_k}(t) := max(\{f_i(x)\} \mid x \in [t_i, t_{i+k}])$; else $c_{p_k}(t) := 0$. Eventually, the goal is to find and define phases in profiles such that the number of phases k and simultaneously the resource waste given by

$$\sum_{i=1}^{k} \int_{t_s}^{t_e} c_{p_k}(x)dx - \int_{t_s}^{t_e} f(x)dx$$

is minimized. First a frequency analysis $\forall P_i$ in T_i could be done. The analysis helps to decide whether by phases anything can be gained and it delivers the interpolation points which could be reused by

12. Conclusion and Outlook

polynomial interpolation to define an approximation function p_i of f_i. Afterwards interpolation points have to be removed such that the resulting polynomial $p'_i(t) \geq f_i(t) \forall t \in T_i$. From this further removals of interpolation points can be done such that the integral increases until the number of points is sufficiently small to define a small number of k phases, see Figure 12.1. Note, during point removal distances of adjacent points must be respect , because of t_{min}. The future intention is finding alternatives, maybe greedy strategies, to identify the envelope of f_i by phases and to evaluate the benefit compared to the original bayesian approach.

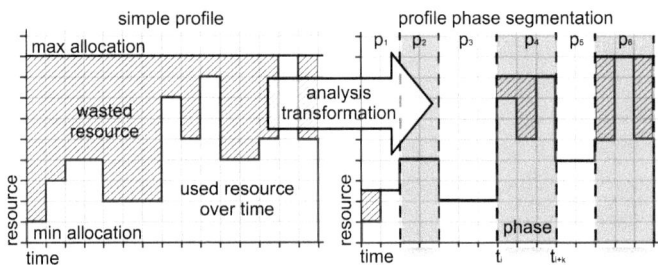

Figure 12.1.: Simplified profile transformation into 6 subsequent phases

With this, the existing FRM approach could be improved by splitting the resource requirements of a profile into phases for more efficient planing of future resource assignments. An approach like Real-time Calculus [TCN00, SPT09] could be used to check schedulability and resource conflicts over time.

Bibliography

[ADG+08] P. Adelt, J. Donoth, J. Gausemeier, J. Geisler, S. Henkler, S. Kahl, B. Klöpper, A. Krupp, E. Münch, S. Oberthür, C. Paiz, H. Podlogar, M. Porrmann, R. Radkowski, C. Romaus, A. Schmidt, B. Schulz, H. Vöcking, U. Witkowski, K. Witting, and O. Znamenshchykov. *Selbstoptimierende Systeme des Maschinenbaus – Definitionen, Anwendungen, Konzepte.*, volume Band 234. HNI-Verlagsschriftenreihe, Paderborn, 2008.

[Agh02] Gul A. Agha. Special issue: Adaptive middleware: Introduction. *Commun. ACM*, 45(6):30–32, 2002.

[Bar06] John Barnes. *Programming in Ada 2005*. Addison Wesley, 2006.

[Bel66] Belady66. A study of replacement algorithms for a virtual-storage computer. *IBM Systems Journal*, 5(2):78–101, 1966.

[BGGO04] Sven Burmester, Matthias Gehrke, Holger Giese, and Simon Oberthür. Making mechatronic agents resource-aware to enable safe dynamic resource allocation. In *4th ACM International Conference on Embedded Software (EMSOFT'2004)*, 27 - 29 September 2004.

[BGO04] Sven Burmester, Holger Giese, and Oliver Oberschelp. Hybrid UML Components for the Design of Complex Self-optimizing Mechatronic Systems. In *Proc. of 1st International Conference on Informatics in Control, Automation and Robotics (ICINCO 2004)*, Setubal, Portugal. IEEE, August 2004.

[BGP+99] Danilo Beuche, Abdelaziz Guerrouat, Holger Papajewski, Wolfgang Schröder-Preikschat, Olaf Spinczyk, and Ute Spinczyk. The pure family of object-oriented operating systems for deeply embedded systems. In *ISORC '99: Proceedings of the 2nd IEEE International Symposium on Object-Oriented Real-Time Distributed Computing*, page 45, Washington, DC, USA, 1999. IEEE Computer Society.

[BGT05] Sven Burmester, Holger Giese, and Matthias Tichy. Model-Driven Development of Reconfigurable Mechatronic Systems with Mechatronic UML. In Uwe Assmann, Arend

Bibliography

                  Rensink, and Mehmet Aksit, editors, *Model Driven Architecture: Foundations and Applications*, volume 3599 of *Lecture Notes in Computer Science*, pages 47–61. Springer Verlag, August 2005.

[BHSC97]   Nina T. Bhatti, Matti A. Hiltunen, Richard D. Schlichting, and Wanda Chiu. Coyote: A system for constructing fine-grain configurable communicationservices. Technical report, University of Arizona, Tucson, AZ, USA, 1997.

[BN02]   Scott A. Brandt and Gary J. Nutt. Flexible soft real-time processing in middleware. *Real-Time Syst.*, 22(1-2):77–118, 2002.

[Bök99]   Carsten Böke. Software Synthesis of Real-Time Communication System Code for Distributed Embedded Applications. In *Proc. of the 6th Annual Australasian Conf. on Parallel and Real-Time Systems (PART)*, Melbourne, Australia, December 1999. IFIP, IEEE.

[Bök03]   Carsten Böke. *Automatic Configuration of Real-Time Operating Systems and Real-Time Communication Systems for Distributed Embedded Applications*. Phd thesis, Faculty of Computer Science, Electrical Engineering, and Mathematics, Paderborn University, Paderborn, Germany, 2003.

[BPB+00]   A. Burns, D. Prasad, A. Bondavalli, F. Di Giandomenico, K. Ramamritham, J. Stankovic, and L. Stringini. The meaning and role of value in scheduling flexible real-time systems. *Journal of Systems Architecture*, 46:305–325, 2000.

[BSI03]   BSI. *British-Adopted European Standard: Railway applications - Communication, signalling and processing systems - Safety related electronic systems for signaling*. The British Standards Institution, 2003.

[BSSZ05]   Böcker, J., Schmidt, A., Schulz, B., and Zimmer, D. Direktantriebe passend ausgewählt - Elektromagnetische Direktantriebe im Vergleich. *Antriebstechnik*, Nr. 2 (spezial):2–6, Februar 2005.

[But04]   Giorgio C. Buttazzo. *Hard Real-time Computing Systems: Predictable Scheduling Algorithms And Applications (Real-Time Systems Series)*. Springer-Verlag Telos, 2004.

[But06]   Giorgio Buttazzo. Research trends in real-time computing for embedded systems. *SIGBED Rev.*, 3(3):1–10, 2006.

Bibliography

[Can29] Walter Bradford Cannon. *Bodily Changes in Pain, Hunger, Fear and Rage: An Account of Recent Research Into the Function of Emotional Excitement.* Appleton-Century-Crofts, 1929.

[CBR02] Ramakrishna Prasad Chivukula, Carsten Böke, and Franz Josef Rammig. Customizing the Configuration Process of an Operating System Using Hierarchy and Clustering. In *Proc. of the 5th IEEE International Symposium on Object-oriented Real-time distributed Computing (ISORC)*, pages 280–287, Crystal City, VA, USA, 29 April – 1 May 2002. IFIP WG 10.5. ISBN 0-7695-1558-4.

[CES71] E. G. Coffman, M. Elphick, and A. Shoshani. System deadlocks. *ACM Comput. Surv.*, 3(2):67–78, 1971.

[Cha91] Eugene Charniak. Bayesian networks without tears. *AI Magazine*, pages 50–63, 1991.

[CHL+03] Anton Cervin, Dan Henriksson, Bo Lincoln, Johan Eker, and Karl-Erik Årzén. How does control timing affect performance? *IEEE Control Systems Magazine*, 23(3):16–30, June 2003.

[DB98] Carsten Ditze and Carsten Böke. Supporting Software Synthesis of Communication Infrastructures for Embedded Real-Time Applications. In *Proc. of the 15th IFAC Workshop on Distributed Computer Control Systems (DCCS)*, Como, Italy, September 1998.

[Der74] Michael L. Dertouzos. Control robotics: The procedural control of physical processes. In *IFIP Congress*, pages 807–813, 1974.

[DIN02a] DIN. *DIN 19226: Control technology; general terms and definitions.* DIN, VDE Verlag Berlin, 2002.

[DIN02b] DIN. *DIN EN 61508: Funktionale Sicherheit sicherheitsbezogener elektrischer/ elektronischer/ programmierbar elektronischer Systeme.* DIN, VDE Verlag Berlin, 2002.

[Dit95] Carsten Ditze. DREAMS – Concepts of a Distributed Real-Time Management System. In *Proc. of the 1995 IFIP/IFAC Workshop on Real-Time Programming (WRTP)*, 1995. (Another copy with quite identical contents appeared in journal *Control Engineering Practice*, Vol. 4 No. 10, 1996.).

[Dit99] Carsten Ditze. *Towards Operating System Synthesis.* Phd thesis, Department of Computer Science, Paderborn University, Paderborn, Germany, 1999.

Bibliography

[Dit00] Carsten Ditze. *Towards Operating System Synthesis*. Dissertation, Universität Paderborn, Heinz Nixdorf Institut, Entwurf Paralleler Systeme, 2000. EUR 35,00, ISBN 3-931466-75-2.

[DM89] Michael L. Dertouzos and Aloysius K. Mok. Multiprocessor on-line scheduling of hard-real-time tasks. In *IEEE Transactions on Software Engineering*, volume 15(12), pages 1497–1506, December 1989.

[EJW+03] Klaus Ecker, David Juedes, Lonnie Welch, David Chelberg, Carl Bruggeman, Frank Drews, David Fleeman, and David Parrott. An optimization framework for dynamic, distributed real-time systems. *International Parallel and Distributed Processing Symposium (IPDPS03)*, page 111b, April 2003.

[Făr06] Emilia Fărcaş. *Scheduling Multi-Mode Real-Time Distributed Components*. PhD thesis, Department of Computer Sciences, University of Salzburg, 2006.

[FBB+97] Bryan Ford, Godmar Back, Greg Benson, Jay Lepreau, Albert Lin, and Olin Shivers. The flux oskit: a substrate for kernel and language research. In *SOSP '97: Proceedings of the sixteenth ACM symposium on Operating systems principles*, pages 38–51, New York, NY, USA, 1997. ACM.

[Fer92] I. A. Ferguson. Touringmachines: Autonomous agents with attitudes. *IEEE Computer*, 25(5):51–55, 1992.

[FGK+04] Ursula Frank, Holger Giese, Florian Klein, Oliver Oberschelp, Andreas Schmidt, Bernd Schulz, Henner Vöcking, and Katrin Witting. *Selbstoptimierende Systeme des Maschinenbaus - Definitionen und Konzepte*. Number Band 155 in HNI-Verlagsschriftenreihe. Bonifatius GmbH, Paderborn, Germany, first edition, November 2004.

[FGL+04] D. Fleeman, M. Gillen, A. Lenharth, M. Delaney, L. Welch, D. Juedes, and C. Liu. Quality-based adaptive resource management architecture (QARMA): a CORBA resource management service. In *Parallel and Distributed Processing Symposium, 2004. Proceedings. 18th International*, 2004.

[GBSO04] Holger Giese, Sven Burmester, Wilhelm Schäfer, and Oliver Oberschelp. Modular Design and Verification of Component-Based Mechatronic Systems with Online-Reconfiguration. In *Proc. of 12th ACM SIGSOFT Foundations of Software Engineering 2004 (FSE 2004), Newport Beach, USA*, pages 179–188. ACM Press, November 2004.

[GFDK08]   Gausemeier, J., Frank, U., Donoth, J., and Kahl, S. Spezifikationstechnik zur beschreibung der prinziplösung selbstoptimierender systeme des maschinenbaus. *Konstruktion*, Teil 1 7/8-2008 und Teil 2 9-2008, 2008.

[GFS06]   Jürgen Gausemeier, Ursula Frank, and Daniel Steffen. Intelligent systems, self-optimizing concepts and structures. In O. Dachtchenko, editor, *Reconfigurable Manufacturing Systems*. Springer-Verlag Berlin, 2006.

[GHH+08]   Holger Giese, Stefan Henkler, Martin Hirsch, Vladimir Roubin, and Matthias Tichy. Modeling techniques for software-intensive systems. In Pierre F. Tiako, editor, *Designing Software-Intensive Systems: Methods and Principles*, Hershey, USA, 2008. IGI Global.

[GKLS07]   J. Gausemeier, S. Kahl, C. Yee Low, and B. Schulz. From the principle solution towards controller design of self-optimizing systems. In J. Gausemeier, F. Rammig, W. Schäfer, A. Trächtler, and Wallaschek, J. (Eds.), editors, *5. Paderborner Workshop "'Entwurf mechatronischer Systeme"', 22.-23. März 2007*, volume Band 210, Paderborn, 2007. HNI-Verlagsschriftenreihe.

[GKP08]   Gausemeier, J., Kahl, S., and Pook, S. From mechatronics to self-optimizing systems. In *7th International Heinz Nixdorf Symposium*, volume Band 223, Paderborn, 2008. HNI-Verlagsschriftenreihe.

[GMM+06]   Holger Giese, Norma Montealegre, Thomas Müller, Simon Oberthür, and Bernd Schulz. Acute stress response for self-optimizing mechatronic systems. In *Proceedings of the IFIP Conference on Biologically Inspired Cooperative Computing*, 21 - 24 August 2006.

[GO03]   Alfonso Gambuzza and Oliver Oberschelp. Distributed modular simulation of mechatronic systems. In *European and Modelling Conference, Naples 2003*, Naples, 2003.

[GOP05]   Björn Griese, Simon Oberthür, and Mario Porrmann. Component case study of a self-optimizing rcos/rtos system: A reconfigurable network service. In *Proceedings of International Embedded Systems Symposium 2005*, Manaos, Brazil, 15 - 17 August 2005.

[GSB+99]   Eran Gabber, Christopher Small, John Bruno, José Brustoloni, and Avi Silberschatz. The pebble component-based operating system. In *ATEC'99: Proceedings of the Annual Technical Conference on 1999 USENIX Annual Technical Conference*, pages 20–20, Berkeley, CA, USA, 1999. USENIX Association.

Bibliography

[GTB+03] H. Giese, M. Tichy, S. Burmester, W. Schäfer, and S. Flake. Towards the compositional verification of real-time uml designs. In *11th ACM SIGSOFT Symposium on Foundations of Software Engineering held jointly with 9th European Software Engineering Conference, September 1-5, 2003, Helsinki, Finland*, pages pp. 38–47, New York, USA, 2003. ACM press.

[GVPR04] Björn Griese, Erik Vonnahme, Mario Porrmann, and Ulrich Rückert. Hardware support for dynamic reconfiguration in reconfigurable soc architectures. In *Proceedings of the International Conference on Field Programmable Logic and its Applications (FPL2004)*, Antwerp, Belgium, 30 August - 1 September 2004.

[GZF+07] Gausemeier, J., Zimmer, D., Frank, U., Klöpper, B., and Schmidt, A. Using active patterns for the conceptual design of self-optimizing systems examplified by an air gap adjustment system. In *ASME International Design Engineering Technical Conferences & Computers and Information in Engineering Conference, 27th Computers and Information in Engineering (CIE'07) Conference, September 4-7, 2007, Las Vegas, Nevada, USA*, 2007.

[HBS+06] Harald Heinecke, Jürgen Bielefeld, Klaus-Peter Schnelle, Nico Maldener, Helmut Fennel, Oliver Weis, Thomas Weber, Jens Ruh, Lennart Lundh, Tomas Sandén, Peter Heitkämper, Robert Rimkus, Jean Leflour, Alain Gilberg, Ulrich Virnich, Stefan Voget, Kenji Nishikawa, Kazuhiro Kajio, Thomas Scharnhorst, and Bernd Kunkel. AUTOSAR – current results and preparations for exploitation. In *Proceedings of the 7th EUROFORUM conference: Software in the vehicle*, May 2006.

[Hec95] D. Heckerman. A tutorial on learning with bayesian networks. Technical report, Microsoft Research, Redmond, Washington, 1995.

[Her04] A Herkersdorf. Towards a framework and a design methodology for autonomic integrated systems. In M Reichert, editor, *Proceedings of the Workshop on Organic Computing*, 2004.

[HF98] Johannes Helander and Alessandro Forin. Mmlite: a highly componentized system architecture. In *EW 8: Proceedings of the 8th ACM SIGOPS European workshop on Support for composing distributed applications*, pages 96–103, New York, NY, USA, 1998. ACM.

[HOG04] Thorsten Hestermeyer, Oliver Oberschelp, and Holger Giese. Structured Information Processing For Self-optimizing Mechatronic Systems. In Helder Araujo, Alves Vieira,

Jose Braz, Bruno Encarnacao, and Marina Carvalho, editors, *Proc. of 1st International Conference on Informatics in Control, Automation and Robotics (ICINCO 2004), Setubal, Portugal*, pages 230–237. INSTICC Press, August 2004.

[Hon98] U. Honekamp. *IPANEMA - Verteilte Echtzeit-Informationsverarbeitung in mechatronischen Systemen*. PhD thesis, Universität Paderborn, Düsseldorf, 1998.

[IEE03] IEEE. *IEEE Standard 1003.13:2003, IEEE Standard for Information Technology-Standardization Application Environment Profile-POSIX Realtime and Embedded Application Support (AEP)*. Institute of Electrical and Electronics Engineers, Inc., 2003.

[IEE04] IEEE. *IEEE Standard 1003.1:2004, IEEE Standard for Information Technology-Portable Operating System Interface (POSIX)-Base Definitions (Volume 1), System Interfaces (Volume 2), Shell and Utilities (Volume 3), and Rationale (Volume 4)*. Institute of Electrical and Electronics Engineers, Inc., 2004.

[ISO95] ISO. *ISO Standard 8652:1995, Information technology – Programming languages - Ada*. International Organization for Standardization, ch. de la Voie-Creuse 1, Case postale 56, CH-1211 Geneva 20, Switzerland, 1995.

[ISO05] ISO. *ISO Standard 17256-3:2005, Road vehicles – Open interface for embedded automotive applications – Part 3: OSEK/VDX Operating System (OS)*. International Organization for Standardization, ch. de la Voie-Creuse 1, Case postale 56, CH-1211 Geneva 20, Switzerland, Nov 2005.

[JG01] Kevin Jeffay and Steve Goddard. Rate-based resource allocation models for embedded systems. In *EMSOFT '01: Proceedings of the First International Workshop on Embedded Software*, pages 204–222, London, UK, 2001. Springer-Verlag.

[JMF+96] Michael B. Jones, Daniel L. McCulley, Alessandro Forin, Paul J. Leach, Daniela Roşu, and Daniel L. Roberts. An overview of the rialto real-time architecture. In *EW 7: Proceedings of the 7th workshop on ACM SIGOPS European workshop*, pages 249–256, New York, NY, USA, 1996. ACM.

[JSMA98] Kevin Jeffay, F. Donelson Smith, Arun Moorthy, and James Anderson. Proportional share scheduling of operating system services for real-time applications. In *In Proceedings of the 19th IEEE Real-Time Systems Symposium*, pages 480–491, 1998.

[KCBC02] Fabio Kon, Fabio Costa, Gordon Blair, and Roy H. Campbell. The case for reflective middleware. *Commun. ACM*, 45(6):33–38, 2002.

[KDK+89] Hermann Kopetz, Andreas Damm, Christian Koza, Marco Mulazzani, Wolfgang Schwabl, Christoph Senft, and Ralph Zainlinger. Distributed fault-tolerant real-time systems: The mars approach. *IEEE Micro*, 9(1):25–40, 1989.

[Ker99] Kernel Specification Working Group. *µiTron4.0 Specification Ver. 4.00.00*, 1999.

[KKS89] D. D. Kandlur, D. L. Kiskis, and K. G. Shin. Hartos: a distributed real-time operating system. *SIGOPS Oper. Syst. Rev.*, 23(3):72–89, 1989.

[KMSM99a] V. Kalogeraki, P. M. Melliar-Smith, and L. E. Moser. Dynamic modeling of replicated objects for dependable soft real-time distributed object systems. *Third IEEE International Symposium on Object-Oriented Real-Time Distributed Computing*, January 1999.

[KMSM99b] V. Kalogeraki, P.M. Melliar-Smith, and L.E. Moser. Using multiple feedback loops for object profiling, scheduling and migration in soft real-time distributed object systems. *IEEE Second International Symposium on Object-Oriented RealTime Distributed Computing*, pages 291–300, May 1999.

[KMSM00] V. Kalogeraki, P. M. Melliar-Smith, and L. E. Moser. Dynamic scheduling for soft real-time distributed object systems. *Third IEEE International Symposium on Object-Oriented Real-Time Distributed Computing*, March 2000.

[KMY+05] Fabio Kon, Jeferson Roberto Marques, Tomonori Yamane, Roy H. Campbell, and M. Dennis Mickunas. Design, implementation, and performance of an automatic configuration service for distributed component systems: Research articles. *Softw. Pract. Exper.*, 35(7):667–703, 2005.

[KPR02] Heiko Kalte, Mario Porrmann, and Ulrich Rückert. A Prototyping Platform for Dynamically Reconfigurable System on Chip Designs. In *Proceedings of the IEEE Workshop Heterogeneous reconfigurable Systems on Chip (SoC)*, Hamburg, Germany, 2002.

[KSC+98] Fabio Kon, Ashish Singhai, Roy H. Campbell, Dulcineia Carvalho, Robert Moore, and Francisco J. Ballesteros. 2k: A reflective, component-based operating system for rapidly changing environments. In S. Demeyer and J. Bosch, editors, *ECOOP Workshops*, volume vol. 1543, pages 388–389, London, 1998. Springer-Verlag.

[LFA+04] Chang Liu, David Fleeman, Eric Aber, Lonnie Welch, and David Juedes. Model-driven resource management for distributed real-time and embedded systems. In *Proceedings of the 10th IEEE Real-Time and Embedded Technology and Applications Symposium (RTAS'04)*, 2004.

[LG99] Hong Li and Roger M. Goodall. Linear and non-linear skyhook damping control laws for active railway suspensions. *Control Engineering Practice*, 7(7):843–850, July 1999.

[LL73] C. L. Liu and James W. Layland. Scheduling algorithms for multiprogramming in a hard-real-time environment. *J. ACM*, 20(1):46–61, 1973.

[LLS+99] Chen Lee, John P. Lehoczky, Daniel P. Siewiorek, Ragunathan Rajkumar, and Jeffery P. Hansen. A scalable solution to the multi-resource qos problem. In *IEEE Real-Time Systems Symposium*, pages 315–326, 1999.

[LO07] Hermann-Simon Lichte and Simon Oberthür. Schedulability criteria and analysis for dynamic and flexible resource management. In *Proceedings of the DASMOD Workshop on Formal Verification of Adaptive Systems*, 2007.

[LRA+02] Joseph P. Loyall, Paul Rubel, Michael Atighetchi, Richard Schantz, and John Zinky. Emerging patterns in adaptive, distributed real-time, embedded middleware. In *9th Conference on Pattern Language of Programs*, 2002.

[MGPK99] David J. Musliner, Robert P. Goldman, Michael J. Pelican, and Kurt D. Krebsbach. Self-Adaptive Software for Hard Real-Time Environments. *IEEE Inteligent Systems*, 14(4), July/August 1999.

[MS04] C. Müller-Schloer. Organic computing: on the feasibility of controlled emergence. In *CODES+ISSS '04: Proceedings of the 2nd IEEE/ACM/IFIP international conference on Hardware/software codesign and system synthesis*, pages 2–5, New York, NY, USA, 2004. ACM.

[Mur02] Kevin P. Murphy. *Dynamic bayesian networks : representation, inference and learning*. PhD thesis, UC Berkeley, 2002.

[Nea03] Richard E. Neapolitan. *Learning Bayesian Networks*. Prentice Hall, April 2003. ISBN 0-130-12534-2.

[OB04] Simon Oberthür and Carsten Böke. Flexible resource management - a framework for self-optimizing real-time systems. In Bernd Kleinjohann, Guang R. Gao, Hermann Kopetz, Lisa Kleinjohann, and Achim Rettberg, editors, *Proceedings of IFIP Working Conference on Distributed and Parallel Embedded Systems (DIPES'04)*. Kluwer Academic Publishers, 23 - 26 August 2004.

Bibliography

[OBG05] Simon Oberthür, Carsten Böke, and Björn Griese. Dynamic online reconfiguration for customizable and self-optimizing operating systems. In *Proceedings of the 5th ACM international conference on Embedded software (EMSOFT'2005)*, pages 335–338, 18 - 22 September 2005. Jersey City, New Jersey.

[OGT+99] Peyman Oreizy, Michael M. Gorlick, Richard N. Taylor, Dennis Heimbigner, Gregory Johnson, Nenad Medvidovic, Alex Quilici, David S. Rosenblum, and Alexander L. Wolf. An Architecture-Based Approach to Self-Adaptive Software. *IEEE Intelligent Systems*, 14(3):54–62, May/June 1999.

[OHC07] Martin Ohlin, Dan Henriksson, and Anton Cervin. *TrueTime 1.5—Reference Manual*, January 2007.

[OR99] S. Oikawa and R. Rajkumar. Portable rk: A portable resource kernel for guaranteed and enforced timing behavior. In *RTAS '99: Proceedings of the Fifth IEEE Real-Time Technology and Applications Symposium*, page 111, Washington, DC, USA, 1999. IEEE Computer Society.

[OZK08] Simon Oberthür, Alex Znamenshchykov, and Benjamin Klöpper. Improved flexible resource management by means of look-ahead scheduling and bayesian forecasting. In Jürgen Gausemeier, Franz Josef Rammig, and Wilhelm Schäfer, editors, *Proceedings of the 7th International Heinz Nixdorf Sysmposium: Self-optimizing Mechatronic Systems*, HNI-Verlagsschriftenreihe, Paderborn, pages 361–376, Paderborn, February 2008.

[PB98] P. Pedro and A. Burns. Schedulability analysis for mode changes in flexible real-timesystems. In *Proceedingsof 10th Euromicro Workshop on Real-Time Systems*, pages 172–179, 1998.

[Pea88] Judea Pearl. *Probabilistic Reasoning in Intelligent Systems : Networks of Plausible Inference*. Morgan Kaufmann, September 1988.

[Pot05] A. Pottharst. *Energieversorgung und Leittechnik einer Anlage mit Linearmotor getriebenen Bahnfahrzeugen*. Dissertation, Fakultät für Maschinenbau, Universität Paderborn, dec 2005.

[RC04] Jorge Real and Alfons Crespo. Mode change protocols for real-time systems: A survey and a new proposal. *Real-Time Syst.*, 26(2):161–197, 2004.

[Rea05] Real-Time for Java Expert Group. *The Real-Time Specification for Java*, 2005.

Bibliography

[RTC92] RTCA. *RTCA/DO-178B: Software Considerations in Airborne Systems and Equipment Certification*. Radio Technical Commission for Aeronautics (RTCA), Washington DC, USA, Dec 1992.

[SAA+04] Lui Sha, Tarek Abdelzaher, Karl-Erik Arzén, Anton Cervin, Theodore Baker, Alan Burns, Giorgio Buttazzo, Marco Caccamo, John Lehoczky, and Aloysius K. Mok. Real time scheduling theory: A historical perspective. *Real-Time Syst.*, 28(2-3):101–155, 2004.

[SAwJ+96] Ion Stoica, Hussein Abdel-wahab, Kevin Jeffay, Sanjoy K. Baruah, Johannes E. Gehrke, and C. Greg Plaxton. A proportional share resource allocation algorithm for real-time, time-shared systems. In *In Proceedings of the 17th IEEE Real-Time Systems Symposium*, pages 288–299, 1996.

[SB96] Marco Spuri and Giorgio C. Buttazzo. Scheduling aperiodic tasks in dynamic priority systems. *Real-Time Systems*, 10(2):179–210, 1996.

[Sch02] Douglas C. Schmidt. Middleware for real-time and embedded systems. *Commun. ACM*, 45(6):43–48, 2002.

[Sch06] Schmidt, A. *Wirkmuster zur Selbstoptimierung – Konstrukte für den Entwurf selbstoptimierender Systeme*. Dissertation, Fakultät für Maschinenbau, Universität Paderborn, 2006. HNI-Verlagsschriftenreihe, Band 204, Paderborn.

[SKB98] Janos Sztipanovits, Gabor Karsai, and Ted Bapty. Self-adaptive software for signal processing. *Commun. ACM*, 41(5):66–73, 1998.

[SMS05] Thorsten Schöler and Christian Müller-Schloer. An observer/controller architecture for adaptive reconfigurable stacks. In *ARCS*, pages 139–153, 2005.

[SPT09] Nikolay Stoimenov, Simon Perathoner, and Lothar Thiele. Reliable mode changes in real-time systems with fixed priority or edf scheduling. In *Proceedings of Design, Automation & Test in Europe (DATE 2009)*, April 2009.

[SR95] John A. Stankovic and Krithi Ramamritham. *A reflective architecture for real-time operating systems*. Prentice-Hall, Inc., Upper Saddle River, NJ, USA, 1995.

[SR04] John A. Stankovic and R. Rajkumar. Real-time operating systems. *Real-Time Syst.*, 28(2-3):237–253, 2004.

Bibliography

[SRN+99] John A. Stankovic, Krithi Ramamritham, Douglas Niehaus, Marty Humphrey, and Gary Wallace. The spring system: Integrated support for complex real-timesystems. *Real-Time Syst.*, 16(2-3):223–251, 1999.

[Str09] Patrik Strömblad. Enea multicore: High performance packet processing enabled with a hybrid smp/amp os technology. Technical report, Enea, 2009.

[Sys08] QNX Software Systems. Qnx industrial software architecture: Rapidly building the systems that make the world work. Technical report, QNX Software Systems, 2008.

[SYS09a] SYSGO AG, 55270 Klein-Winternheim, Deutschland. *Datasheet ELinOS 5.0 - Industrial Grade Linux*, 2009.

[SYS09b] SYSGO AG, 55270 Klein-Winternheim, Deutschland. *Datasheet PikeOS*, 2009.

[Sys09c] Wind River Systems. Wind river vxworks platforms 3.7, Jan 2009.

[Tan08] Andrew S. Tanenbaum. *Modern Operating Systems*. Prentice Hall, third edition, 11 2008.

[TCN00] Lothar Thiele, Samarjit Chakraborty, and Martin Naedele. Real-time calculus for scheduling hard real-time systems. In *in ISCAS*, pages 101–104, 2000.

[TM89] H. Tokuda and C. W. Mercer. Arts: a distributed real-time kernel. *SIGOPS Oper. Syst. Rev.*, 23(3):29–53, 1989.

[TMV06] A. Trachtler, E. Munch, and H. Vocking. Iterative learning and Self-Optimization techniques for the innovative Railcab-System. In *IEEE Industrial Electronics, IECON 2006 - 32nd Annual Conference on*, pages 4683–4688, 2006.

[TNR90] Hideyuki Tokuda, Tatsuo Nakajima, and Prithvi Rao. Real-time Mach: Towards a predictable real-time system. In *Proceedings of the Usenix Mach Workshop*, pages 73–82. USENIX Association, 1990.

[VASP09] G. Vouros, A. Artikis, K. Stathis, and J. Pitt, editors. *Organized Adaption in Multi-Agent Systems - First International Workshop, OAMAS 2008, Estoril, Portugal, May 13, 2008. Revised and Invited Papers*, volume 5368 of *Lecture Notes in Artificial Intelligence*. Springer, 2009.

[VD98] Jacques Ferber Vincent Decugis. Action selection in an autonomous agent with a hierarchical distributed reactive planning architecture. In *Proceedings of the second international conference on Autonomous agents*, pages 354–361. ACM Press, 1998.

Bibliography

[VGPR04] Erik Vonnahme, Björn Griese, Mario Porrmann, and Ulrich Rückert. Dynamic reconfiguration of real-time network interfaces. In *Proceedings of the 4th International Conference on Parallel Computing in Electrical Engineering (PARELEC 2004)*, pages 376–379, Dresden, Germany, 7 - 10 September 2004.

[VT08] H. Vöcking and A. Trächtler. Self-optimization of an active suspension system regarding energy requirements. In *International Conference on Control, Automation and Systems 2008 (ICCAS 2008), October 14-17, 2008, Seoul*, 2008. akzeptiert.

[Wir04] Martin Wirsing, editor. *Report on the EU/NSF Strategic Workshop on Engineering Software-Intensive Systems*, Edinburgh, GB, May 2004.

[WSD+08] Katrin Witting, Bernd Schulz, Michael Dellnitz, Joachim Böcker, and Norbert Fröhleke. A new approach for online multiobjective optimization of mechatronic systems. *International Journal on Software Tools for Technology Transfer (STTT)*, 10(3):223–231, June 2008.

[Yag01] Karim Yaghmour. The real-time application interface. In *Proceedings of the 2001 Linux Symposium*, 2001.

[Yok92] Yasuhiko Yokote. The apertos reflective operating system: the concept and its implementation. In *OOPSLA '92: conference proceedings on Object-oriented programming systems, languages, and applications*, pages 414–434, New York, NY, USA, 1992. ACM.

I want morebooks!

Buy your books fast and straightforward online - at one of world's fastest growing online book stores! Environmentally sound due to Print-on-Demand technologies.

Buy your books online at
www.morebooks.shop

Kaufen Sie Ihre Bücher schnell und unkompliziert online – auf einer der am schnellsten wachsenden Buchhandelsplattformen weltweit! Dank Print-On-Demand umwelt- und ressourcenschonend produziert.

Bücher schneller online kaufen
www.morebooks.shop

KS OmniScriptum Publishing
Brivibas gatve 197
LV-1039 Riga, Latvia
Telefax: +371 686 204 55

info@omniscriptum.com
www.omniscriptum.com

Printed by Books on Demand GmbH, Norderstedt / Germany